To Bishop Beesner
Best wishes
and prayers.
Mary Higbee

Lessons From Afar

Mary Higbee

ISBN-13:
978-1537667836

ISBN-10:
1537667831

Cover design by Craig Johnson, JTE Photography

Lessons from Afar is dedicated to Darryl and Jennifer Ernst, Founders of Hope and Resurrection Secondary School. For their vision and commitment in making a dream come true in South Sudan.

Contents

INTRODUCTION

New experiences and difficult challenges often result in the development and growth of spiritual maturity. *Lessons from Afar* is about such experiences and challenges, and what I learned from them when my husband, Jim, and I served nine months as missionaries in Southern Sudan. In the rural village of Atiaba, we worked to open a newly built school named Hope and Resurrection Secondary.

We lived for a school year in Southern Sudan[1] in 2008 during the small window of time between the end of a twenty-three-year long civil war and the violence and civil unrest that began in December 2013. Jim and I are among a limited number of foreign visitors that experienced the relatively peaceful and hopeful time that occurred during this period. Our stories of Southern Sudan need telling, for to judge the value of this culture by the horrific news stories of last few years is not to know the whole truth

---

[1] In the Comprehensive Peace Agreement of 2005, Sudan was separated into Northern and Southern Sudan. In 2011 Southern Sudan became the independent nation of South Sudan. Southern Sudan will be the name used throughout most of this book since the time frame covered is 2008 before South Sudan had become an independent nation.

of people who love their families, want progress, and long for leadership that is not corrupt.

My missionary experiences do not always make pretty stories. As ready and committed as I believed I was when Jim and I boarded the plane for Africa, I often stumbled as I tried to live out the mission to help begin a secondary school. Through my stumbling, I learned to think and live in ways that were not about my comfort and convenience but were about how to develop the resilience to fall and, with God's help, to get up again.

In the first months after Jim and I returned to the United States from Southern Sudan, I found it difficult to know how to explain the complexity of all that had occurred in my head and heart. It was not until we visited a rainforest exhibit at the National Academy of Sciences in San Francisco that I found a precise metaphor which eloquently expressed my transformation.

The rainforest exhibit provided information about light gaps. A light gap occurs in a rainforest when a large canopy tree dies and falls, and in the tree's absence, shafts of light penetrate deep into the interior of the forest floor where limited light has been. The light gap facilitates a hothouse of new life, as plants compete for the nutrients provided by the fallen tree and take advantage of the possibilities for growth that the light offers.

Standing there in the Academy of Sciences Museum, I re-read the light gap information several times, seeing the similarities between the natural world and my internal landscape of thoughts and feelings while in Southern Sudan. Many of my preconceived notions of missionary life and some long-held judgments perished in the same way that the fallen canopy tree dies in the rainforest. The people I met and the things I learned on the other side of the world served as my "light gap" by providing opportunities for discovery and understanding about myself, others, and God.

Introduction

In *Lessons from Afar,* I relate my stories through the lenses of the many life lessons that awaited me in Southern Sudan. These life lessons were not new to me. They had been with me in all kinds of circumstances, yet I had not always integrated what I learned into my life in a lasting way. Living and working in a culture that was not my own made the lessons about trust, vulnerability, humility, perseverance, and non-judgment immediate and necessary for my emotional and spiritual well-being.

I invite you to accompany me as I recount my experiences in Southern Sudan in *Lessons from Afar.* I look forward to introducing you to some of the students of the first class of Hope and Resurrection Secondary and letting you glimpse the culture of the newest country in the world. This invitation includes the opportunity to pursue your own spiritual understanding by reflecting on the events of your life and Scripture passages.

On the other side of the world, amid scarcity and need, I experienced God's generosity and a life-affirming purpose for me. Which brings us to the question that is at the center of this book: Can the lessons taught to me by God and the Dinka people of Southern Sudan be brought home to the United States for a life that is more abundant and generous? Please join me in seeking answers to that question.

Sincerely,

Mary Higbee

OVERVIEW OF *Lessons from Afar*

My missionary experiences inspired this book. *Lessons from Afar* provides an unusual backdrop for its stories, and the stories illustrate lessons about God and the human spirit that couldn't be missed or dismissed when learned in the African culture of Southern Sudan.

If you have ever wondered what life in the mission field is like, this book will let you sample some of the experiences of a missionary couple, although *Lessons* is more than a memoir. The questions and activity at the end of each chapter invite you to consider how trust, humility, vulnerability, gratitude, and perseverance are reflected in your daily life. The invitation includes discovering possible ways that you can reflect on prayer, actions, and attitudes that will support your spiritual growth and perhaps reveal God's unique call to you.

Lessons from Afar can be enjoyed as an individual or in a small group book study. If you are reading this book on your own, complete the activity and questions after reading each chapter. I suggest that you slow down and take your time in considering how the chapter's theme can be applied to the circumstances of your life. Record your thoughts in a dedicated notebook or journal. If you have a friend, family member, or spiritual director with whom you can share your insights and personal stories, your experience will be enhanced.

If *Lessons from Afar* is used as a small group study, an hour or an hour and a half is the suggested meeting time. Each person in the group will need a copy of *Lessons* and a dedicated notebook or journal for recording their thoughts and ideas each week. A check-in question starts each meeting. The question provides an opportunity for spiritual storytelling and connects the theme of the chapter to the lives of the members of the group. As part of the meeting, there is quiet time set aside to think and write about any insights that have been gained. A detailed Facilitator's Guide for leading a group study is located at the end of the book.

GOD SHAPING OUR EXPERIENCES

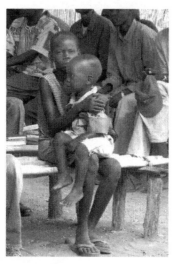

CHAPTER 1

Being Called—A Compelling Invitation

Isaiah 6:8—Then I heard the voice of the Lord saying, "Whom shall I send? And who will go for us?" And I said, "Here am I. Send me!"

1 Peter 4:10—Each of you should use whatever gift you have received to serve others, as faithful stewards of God's grace in its various forms.

How does a California middle school English teacher find herself in a rural Southern Sudan village to open a secondary school? The short, concise answer to that question is "God," but let me explain with a few more details. My passion for education merged with an unrelenting sense that the time to act was now and a window of opportunity was at hand for something extraordinary. The combination of those ideas became like a neon sign inside my head blinking in big, hot pink letters "be a missionary."

At first glance, this idea to be a missionary seemed like a sudden revelation, but tracing back through decades I can pinpoint the germination of the idea to my fifth-grade school year. In a small country school outside of Peoria, Illinois, I read in a *Weekly Reader* about Albert Schweitzer and his hospital in Africa. Albert Schweitzer interested me because I had already developed a keen curiosity about people in other parts of the world. I regarded him as a hero because of Dr. Schweitzer's willingness to take his knowledge and skills as a doctor to a far-off place that needed them. In the following years of my young adulthood, it appears that I forgot my hero and his inspirational work, but a closer look reveals experiences and interests that over decades guided me to discover the path to being a missionary.

In our early thirties, Jim and I experienced what we believe was a call from God to the mission field, but in this case, the location was close to home. This "call" came on a Sunday morning in 1979 at our church in Northern California. The sermon included our pastor sharing his vision for our congregation to sponsor a Cambodian family, and Church World Service's appeal to churches to help resettle families who were fleeing their war-torn countries and being allowed to immigrate to the United States.

Our pastor shared the need for donations of money and people willing to work with the family assigned to our church. Jim and I did not have a large income, but we decided to find a way to donate funds to the cause. Through a series of circumstances, those who were to chair the resettlement of the refugee family could not do so. Jim and I realized that we were not being called to give money but to give of ourselves because almost overnight I was overseeing the resettlement. Initially, I was nervous because I believed that I did not have the experience or qualifications to take on such a big job.

Matthew 19:26

The Chhen family of twelve arrived in September and stayed temporarily with a couple who had a big home. I went to meet them for the first time and took my son, Matthew, with me. The Chhen family knew very little English, and I worried about how I was going to communicate with them. Matthew observed the Chhen family for a couple of minutes, then stepped forward. With the exuberant confidence of a six-year-old who loves the world, he invited them to come to his house for a visit. Although the Chhens did not understand Matthew's words, they comprehended his welcome. The Chhens responded with smiles, and the mother reached out to embrace Matthew. My nervousness vanished, and I stopped second guessing my qualifications to care for this family.

Matthew and his pre-school aged brother, Mark, and the young children of the Chhen family played together with toy cars, my blonde sons' heads leaning close to the dark-haired heads of their new playmates, and all of them becoming a chorus of car engine noises. The women in the family taught me how to make fried rice, and in turn, I mentored them on how to do things like navigating an American supermarket and enrolling the children in school. One of the things I remember about the first days of the re-settlement of the Chhen family was pantomiming the things we needed to communicate. These sessions required patience and a sense of humor since most exchanges took several attempts. When at last we understood, we hugged each other in triumph, grinning broadly with much nodding of our heads.

I loved having my family's world expand through the friendship of the Chhen family. The cultural exchange was rich and exciting to me. I discovered that the things that I had regarded as being unimportant were exactly what was helpful in the resettlement. My being a mother of young children, a shopper who knew the best places for bargains, a patient teacher, and one who appreciated other cultures was the right combination for being the Chhens' mentor. Jim and I believe it was God who inspired our willingness to answer the call to help with the re-settlement the Chhen family. At the time, we could not know the experience would someday be a cornerstone for our choosing to be missionaries.

Years later when Matthew and Mark were teens, I returned to college to complete the fifth year of teacher training. My first teaching job was in an eighth grade English and history classroom populated with the first generation of children of Hmong immigrants to this country. These young people had been infants in their mothers' arms when their families escaped to refugee camps. Their stories told of the fear and suffering that their families experienced in life and death circumstances before coming to the United States. I utilized all I had learned from my certification classes to be a teacher of second language learners, especially the idea of creating a classroom culture that was safe and nurturing.

One day, a lunchtime performance featured Hmong dancing, and my classroom became the dressing room for the Hmong girls to change into their traditional dresses of full pleated skirts and beautiful scarves crossed in front and tucked into wide cummerbunds.

"My mother has a dress for you to wear today if you want to dress like us," a student told me. The Hmong mothers knew no English, but I understood to stand with outstretched arms while they wrapped the fabric around me for my skirt and arranged the elaborate headwear. When they had pinned and smoothed my costume, I looked in a mirror, while the girls gathered around me to assure me I looked beautiful. My reflection showed my transformation on the outside, but I knew I was transformed on the inside, as well, from having had the opportunity to know and care for my Hmong students.

These events and others accumulated through time to shape my worldview. I believe that human potential is one of the greatest resources on Earth. This belief began with my girlhood curiosity about other cultures and continued with the friendship of the Chhen family. The idea of the worth of each person developed fully as a teacher of the Hmong and Hispanic students, who needed my help to bridge from the culture of their birth to their living in the United States. My education is precious to me and has opened many doors, including realizing my dream of being a teacher. I see education as one of the ways to empower people to be the best they can be.

Jim and I had each grown up attending church, and we continued to do so with our family of four. Over decades, I listened to many sermons, joined Bible studies, read Christian books, and became a member of the Society of Companions of the Holy Cross. I increasingly asked myself the question found in the baptismal covenant of the Episcopal prayer book, "Will you strive for justice and peace among all people, and respect the dignity of every human being?" I wanted to be an agent of peace and justice. I thought I was doing so in my classroom but wondered how I could do so in a more expansive way.

I describe my life as one of good fortune, both in the past and present, for I have everything that is dear to me in the way of people and vocation. I believe in whatever form our good fortune takes, it is not meant to stop with us but to pass on. Our talents and abilities are given to us to share, and in return, we experience the deep satisfaction that comes from having a meaningful purpose and a connection to others. I knew I had something to pass on through the field of education.

These thoughts became a tangible longing to be in the mission field. This yearning was inconvenient, and at first, I did my best to ignore it. Recently retired from a career with the State of California, Jim was enjoying designing and making furniture. I liked the school where I taught and my seventh grade English students. Our two adult sons were leading lives that made them happy. We lived in a comfortable house with a view of the distant Sierra Nevada Mountains. The circumstances of my life should have been enough to satisfy me, yet the restlessness would not be stilled.

I proposed to Jim that we go on a week-long mission trip to Honduras with some members of our church. "Can we go and see how it feels to be in a developing country surrounded by poverty and if there is something we can do to help?" Jim agreed to go, and I resisted saying too much more. I was sure if I was meant to be a missionary, then Jim needed to be a part of it. If it were a call from God, then Jim would know without my pressuring him.

Watching a ragged, barefoot young Honduran boy and his even smaller sister run in and out of traffic to sell pineapples to people in passing cars is the image that will always stay with us from the trip to Honduras. Combined with other scenes during the trip, we discerned a compelling call to action. We witnessed ways we might serve others using our life experiences and education. On the plane traveling home, Jim told me that he would be interested in investigating missionary opportunities.

During the next year, we researched ways to enter the mission field and were accepted into a program with Episcopal Church to be volunteer missionaries. I retired early from teaching, and we attended a two-week missionary training. Jim and I were offered a mission post in Jerusalem to work with the Anglican bishop in his office as administrative support. It was an incredible opportunity but not what we had envisioned.

To help with our decision about accepting or declining the Jerusalem post, I talked with an Episcopal priest who had just returned from serving in Jerusalem. After our discussion, he said to me, "Mary, I believe your call to the mission field is a true one, and that God will bless whatever mission post you choose." This priest encouraged me to see the call to the mission field as an invitation to join my passions and abilities with God's mission of grace and mercy in the world. The interview renewed Jim's and my trust in our discernment that God was calling us to work in education.

Within a few days of declining the assignment to Jerusalem, we received news that a nonprofit organization, Hope for Humanity based in Richmond, Virginia, was seeking someone to open a newly built secondary school in rural Southern Sudan. Jim took the phone call about the school, and he tells how he knew immediately that the long-awaited news had finally arrived.

The facts interested us: Southern Sudan was only three years out of a twenty-three-year long civil war, life expectancy was 47 years, and literacy rate was less than fifteen percent. The new school was named Hope and Resurrection Secondary School and located in a rural village with no electricity, mail service, or cell phone towers. The plan for the school was to open with a freshmen class and add a class level each year after that. The school was to serve the people of the Dinka tribe, whose religions were Christian and animist.

It did not make worldly sense that Jim and I would reject living in a lovely furnished apartment in the compound of the Anglican Bishop of Jerusalem but readily embraced the idea of going to Southern Sudan. Over creature comforts, we chose Southern Sudan which meant that we would be pumping our water at a village well, living in the heat near the Equator, and having limited resources and means of communication.

Recognizing a call to serve God and others is like connecting dots. We each have unique personalities which shape the interests we develop. We have special abilities that are innately our own, and those abilities influence the work and play we choose. The way we see and interact with the world depends on the sum total of all we are and have experienced. As a result, different situations and needs move us to compassion and action. When all that is unique within us meets a need for which we have interest and passion, the dots are connected, and a call to mission is born.

Matthew 19:26

The call to the mission field in Southern Sudan will always be one of the most profound experiences of my life, but we don't necessarily have to go to the other side of the world to act on a call from God. When we are thoughtful about our gifts and passions and alert to the situations around us, the possibilities present themselves in our families, neighborhoods, churches, and beyond. Accepting a call to action has outcomes we can't possibly imagine--it is life in amazing color and high definition.

Relating the chapter's theme to your life: We learn new things when we move out of our comfort zone. Recall a time that you left a place where you were comfortable to go somewhere which was much different? What lesson(s) did you learn from the experience?

CHAPTER 1

QUESTIONS AND ACTIVITIES

If you are meeting with a group, take turns relating your personal story to one another that answers the following question. If you are reading on your own, record your story in your notebook.

Relating the chapter's theme to your life: We learn new things when we move out of our comfort zone. Recall a time that you left a place where you were comfortable to go somewhere which was much different? What lesson(s) did you learn from the experience?

Chapter 1 shares examples about how a lifetime of experiences, interests, and abilities was used by God to shape the desire to serve others.

Isaiah 6:8—*Then I heard the voice of the Lord saying, "Whom shall I send? And who will go for us?" And I said, "Here am I. Send me!"*

1 Peter 4:10—*Each of you should use whatever gift you have received to serve others, as faithful stewards of God's grace in its various forms.*

The verse from Isaiah is clear that a call from God is real, and each of us has the choice not to respond or to do as the speaker did by saying, *"Here am I. Send me!"* It says in 1 Peter that God-given gifts are meant to be used to serve others and enable us to be a part of God's ever-unfolding mission in the world. Throughout the span of each of our lives, we experience different calls to serve God and others. Our personal history combined with our abilities, talents, and personality merge to create ongoing opportunities for service.

The chapter's activity will help in understanding past and present calls to serve God and others and can possibly identify future calls to serve in ways that will be fulfilling and joyful. During the next week, continue this activity and write in your journal to develop your ideas.

Part 1

In your notebook record your thoughts by creating a mind map or web. See the following example for creating mind map of five circles. Label your mind map like the example.

Mind maps or webs are a way to gather and recall information quickly. They are not linear, so when making a mind map, move from topic to topic and back again in any order. Add circles and connecting lines radiating from each main circle to record your responses. Don't edit your thoughts—record whatever comes to mind. Do not be modest.

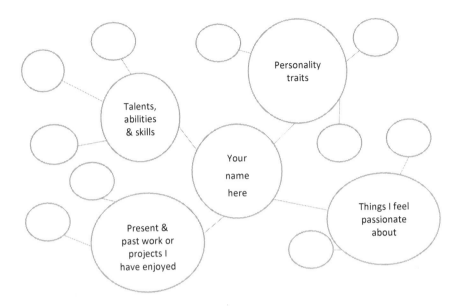

Talent, abilities, and skills - This can include things like being musical, able to work with animals, having writing or math abilities, having speaking and acting talent, being skilled in the culinary arts, artistic talent, knowing how to utilize technology, and on and on.

Personality Traits - This can include things like being strategic, compassionate, honest, creative, thoughtful, encouraging, pastoral, and so on.

Past or present work or projects I have enjoyed – This can include your secular work, hobbies, things done in the context of your home, or ministries in the church or for charities.

Passions - This can include things like your family's welfare, the environment, animals, education, medical research, saving endangered species, veteran issues, women's issues, homelessness, human trafficking and on and on.

Part 2

Study your completed mind map. You have created a visual of how your personality, abilities, and experiences relate to the things which have your interest and attention. Notice the things you recorded for your passions and consider if there is a correlation between what you listed as your passions and the other areas of your mind map.

- Ask how the projects and work you enjoy can support some of the areas about which you feel passionate.
- Assess your talents, skills, and abilities and decide which ones would be helpful if you offered your services in some of the areas of your passions.
- Review your personality traits and decide which ones would be helpful if you offered your services in some of the areas of your passions.
- What obstacles are in the way of your acting on some of your passions? How can you pray and think about the obstacles?

Part 3

Re-read *1 Peter 4:10 - Each of you should use whatever gift you have received to serve others, as faithful stewards of God's grace in its various forms.*

- In what ways does the information on your mind map affirm how you are using your gifts now and in the past in the service of others?
- Are there any surprises or connections that you have not previously made about serving God and others that would be fulfilling and suit your unique talents and personality?
- Did you discover any possibilities for the future (perhaps even in another season of your life)?

If you are working on your own, re-read what you have written. Sharing your thoughts gained from the activity and questions with a friend is a further way to explore your ideas and get feedback.

If you are working in a small group, meet back in your group and as each person is comfortable, share any thoughts and insights. End the meeting with prayer and affirmation for the insights the group brought forward.

During the next week, review your reflections and add any further insights to your journal.

CHAPTER 2

Trust—Not the Beginning We Envisioned

Isaiah 12:2—*Surely God is my salvation; I will trust and not be afraid. The Lord, the Lord himself is my strength and my defense; he has become my salvation."*

Philippians 4:6—*Do not be anxious about anything, but in every situation, by prayer and petition, with thanksgiving, present your requests to God. And the peace of God, which transcends all understanding, will guard your hearts and your minds in Christ Jesus.*

John 20:19-22—*On the evening of that first day of the week, when the disciples were together, with the doors locked for fear of the Jewish leaders Jesus came and stood among them and said, "Peace be with you!" As the Father has sent me, I am sending you." And with that he breathed on them and said, "Receive the Holy Spirit."*

On February 18, 2008, Jim and I departed the United States for Kampala, Uganda. The flight from San Francisco marked the beginning of a year's mission to open Hope and Resurrection Secondary School in rural

Southern Sudan. We boarded the plane and collapsed from the collective fatigue and excitement of the hectic months of preparation for leaving our life's activities, and family and friends. Jim and I had worked through details about mail, financial matters, and finding a person who wanted to house sit for us. We had researched education in Africa and communicated daily with Jennifer and Darryl Ernst, founders of Hope for Humanity, the organization that had built the school and would be funding its operation. It was surrealistic to be strapped into the airplane seat and be required to sit there quietly after so many months of frenzied activity. To finally be on our way was exhilarating.

We arrived in Kampala, Uganda and spent the next eighteen days trying to accomplish all the business involved in getting visas, purchasing instructional and household supplies, and hiring teachers. None of these things were available in Southern Sudan which had been depleted of all resources during the two decades of civil war. What we bought in Kampala would have to last for an entire school year in Southern Sudan; anticipating those needs and locating the supplies was a challenge. Each day, we learned how to find what we needed in an African city which was like a crazy quilt with squares of a progressive, modern city next to patches of slums whose citizens lead desperate lives to survive. In a blog[2] I wrote:

Conducting business in Africa is not according to the Western multi-tasking we are used to, so buying things like textbooks or lab supplies take most of the day rather than being a quick purchase. There are a few big stores, but most of the things we have bought came from dusty little shops that at first did not look promising. We bought a used four-wheel-drive Toyota pickup truck for the

[2] Higbee, Mary et al. "Higbees In Southern Sudan". Higbees.blogspot.com. N.p. 2008

school, and that experience was a complicated one. We have everything possible–large bags of rice and maize, clothespins, generators, and beds and mattresses to furnish the teachers' rooms–you name it.

The most difficult challenge has been to hire qualified teachers. We found an excellent man for the business, geography, and biology classes, but a combination math and chemistry teacher is not easy to find. Not only does the candidate need to be qualified, but also an adventurer who would like to come to Southern Sudan.

The difficulty of accomplishing tasks quickly or at all in a developing country sank in as we did business in Kampala. Amid the long, tiring days of conducting business and making decisions, we appreciated the good things that occurred. Encouraging events like someone's help in getting Sudanese visas, finding a teacher who wanted to join us in Southern Sudan, or worshipping with over a thousand people in the Anglican Cathedral each Sunday balanced the situations that felt tense and frustrating. I wrote in my journal that Jim and I were happy to leave Kampala for Southern Sudan. Because of our preliminary visit three months earlier to Rumbek, the town nearest to the village of Atiaba and the school, I believed we knew what to expect. The dirt airstrip and the dusty marketplace with its cooking pots, sacks of maize flour and diesel fuel in soda pop bottles wouldn't be a surprise. We looked forward to beginning the actual work of setting up Hope and Resurrection Secondary School. Mary Higbee, the passionate educator, was ready to go.

As the little plane taxied to a stop in Rumbek, we spotted the assistant bishop waiting for us on the edge of the airstrip. There is no way to ease into Rumbek for the moment the plane doors open, the intense heat and blowing red dust greet you, as well as many outstretched hands of welcome. The assistant bishop took us to the compound where we would be staying until the truck with all the supplies for the school arrived from Uganda. When we had visited Rumbek the previous November, we stayed in a compound equipped with comfortable beds, electric fans, and Western-style bathrooms. Jim and I decided we were not tourists, and our missionary status and tight budget determined that we stay in African accommodations. It took only a few minutes and some joking comments to recover from being deposited in a tiny thatched roof hut with sagging beds, holes in the mosquito netting, and no electricity. We remained positive even after looking at the primitive outhouses and bathing accommodations. Having a shower meant filling a basin with cloudy water from a collection tank, taking it into a small structure that served as a bathhouse, and using a cup to pour water on yourself. "After all," we said to each other, "weren't we expecting challenging conditions?"

What we weren't expecting was the waiting because our Western culture hadn't groomed us to feel patient while waiting for something to happen. That first afternoon, we were waiting for someone to take us to our formal visit with the Episcopal bishop for whom we now worked. We moved the plastic chairs from our hut and sat outside and watched goats nibble the last blades of grass growing on the hard-packed red dirt. Three hot, boring hours of dozing against our will and waking up very groggy went by before someone came to take us to the bishop. Gladly, we walked the few blocks to the bishop's compound because in our minds this visit would launch the beginning of our mission to open Hope and Resurrection Secondary School.

The bishop was not a stranger to us because we had met him the previous November when we had visited Southern Sudan to meet key people connected with the opening of the school. When Jim and I left the bishop in November after several hours of conversation and notetaking, we felt sure we understood his priorities concerning the school and how we should proceed. We approached today's interview with the bishop as a formality. We thought we already knew his wishes about Hope and Resurrection Secondary and had come prepared to act on those desires.

The partial walls of a bombed house leftover from the recent civil war dominated the space inside the bishop's fenced compound. It reminded me of a stage set designed to convey to the audience the horrible deeds that had occurred before the curtain went up. The bishop met with people under a mango tree which provided an irregular circle of shade that was cool even on the hottest days. Waiting people filled all the plastic chairs. A ceremony resembling musical chairs began immediately with two people giving up their chairs for us as dictated by Dinka etiquette. We sat down and waited for the bishop's attention and our turn to speak. It was like sitting in a doctor's waiting room, as I studied the people and wondered about the purpose of their visit. Unlike a medical waiting room, the conversations with the bishop did not seem to offer much privacy. Jim and I sat side by side but did not speak to one another, so intent and alert we each were to catch clues as to how we should behave.

When our turn came, we moved our chairs next the bishop's chair. The conversation that unfolded revealed things had changed since our meeting three months ago. The bishop was negative about the location of the school which he now believed was in the wrong place. He predicted not many students would show up. Also, he told us there was no headmaster candidate to be found, even though during the discussion three months ago, we had been assured this would not pose a problem. I felt my stomach knot since this latest news negated the information on which we had based many of our plans and decisions for the school. We also learned the government exit exam for eighth graders which should have been given months before, had just been given, and these exams were not yet marked. Not having the scores meant we did not have the exam results which were to be our criteria for admission into freshman class (called Senior 1) at Hope and Resurrection Secondary School.

An internal argument started in my head with the bishop about why things had changed so much in just a few months. It was all I could do to sit in my chair and keep my hands in my lap and my mouth closed. Afterward, I realized the scene with the bishop was reminiscent of an early TV show I had watched when I was a little girl. The show was called "Beat the Clock," and week after week the show's pattern was the same. A married couple was given a challenging task to complete in a certain amount of time which usually involved the husband getting hit with cream pies. At the last minute, they told the wife that the already tricky stunt would have to be done blindfolded. The audience would groan their sympathy which made me feel nervous for these people on the little black and white TV screen. The bishop's news was the equivalent of telling us that the task of opening a secondary school would have challenges equal to being a blindfolded and competing against a ticking clock.

I had not presumed to know what the next nine months would bring, but I had counted on some control of the opening of Hope and Resurrection Secondary School based on what I had learned from the bishop three months earlier. Anxiety replaced the optimism I had felt when I exited the plane just hours before. I risked a glance at Jim because I wondered what he was thinking about all the latest information dumped in our laps during the last few minutes. Just under the surface of the calmness that we both were striving to master on the spot, I glimpsed a flicker of determination in Jim and seeing that barely perceptible set of his jaw inspired me to take a deep breath and relax a little. The challenges of opening Hope and Resurrection Secondary School were beginning to exert themselves in real ways. The conversation under the bishop's mango tree revealed that no amount of planning could have prepared us for what was ahead.

The following Monday morning, I sat under a neem tree in the grassless compound yard of the place where we were staying in Rumbek. Jim was off doing an errand, and time seemed to stand still in the oppressive heat. I turned to my journal and began enlarging my new theory on the lack of control I had to open a secondary school.

Monday, March 16, 2008 – Under a neem tree, mid-morning, Rumbek, Southern Sudan:

Perhaps only an English teacher would see this experience so far as if it was a fictional fantasy with all the elements of a hero's quest--a missionary's version of Star Wars or Beowulf, but that is the way I saw it clearly in the middle of the night.

My life in California afforded me an expansive sense of control over my time and activities. How different it is to be in a plastic chair under a neem tree in Rumbek. The day is heating up and already the plastic chair and I have chased the declining shade in a circle. There is no electricity, so none of our gadgets can be charged and lay lifeless on the sagging table in our room. They mock us for depending on them. We have no transportation, and any expedition outside the compound holds the danger of heat stroke and blisters. I feel like a character in a story who has no idea what will happen on the next page.

The lack of control hits the hardest at first light. Early morning is my favorite time of the day when I am still a bit sleepy but rested, and the day stretches before me like a blank canvas. I used to plan my day each morning in my California bedroom when I was master of the hours before me, but here in Southern Sudan, I am the master of very little. In place of plans, I now entertain possibilities but as lightly as a butterfly lighting on a petal. I review the lessons of the last few weeks which are to plan loosely, count on nothing until it actually happens, and be prepared to be surprised.

Has the plot emerged for you? A missionary couple comes to Southern Sudan to help start a secondary school. They are sincere but naïve. Their faith is as strong as it can be for people who have not had to come through any great tests. They bring talents developed over a lifetime and an earnest desire to be of help. Yet nothing prepares them for the combination of the heat and poverty and a way of doing things that seem inefficient. Any sense of empowerment felt in the United States is at loose ends in Africa. Life slows down to almost a standstill, and they accomplish very little in a day. The task of opening a secondary school looms large. Unlike a fictional hero's quest, Mary and James do not have a treasure map, key, or magic potion. They do have a guide if they will stop and listen. They will have rest if they claim the quiet days rather than fight them. Is there room for God in this fantasy? Remember the lessons are to plan loosely, count on nothing until it actually happens, and be prepared for surprises. God, of course, is in the surprises.

The act of writing that journal entry is vivid. I was not with Jim because of a large blister on my left foot from walking around Rumbek the last two days. The only shoes I could wear were Jim's size eleven flip-flops, and I wondered if I would have to wear the too-big flip-flops for the next nine months. I wrote with thought and care because I wanted to fill up some of the time that was passing so slowly. I recalled teaching my American seventh-grade students about a hero's quest through the reading of Robert Nye's version of *Beowulf*[3] and revisiting the plots of movies like *Star Wars* and *Indiana Jones*. The points of a hero's quest that applied to my situation were the daunting obstacles that had to be encountered and conquered, and the knowledge that the final test was not an external one but an internal struggle for truth.

When I got to the end of my journal entry, I raced to finish the thought—God is in the surprises. I was relieved at how I ended my journal entry, almost as if it was a new thought, which it wasn't it. There had been many times when I had experienced God's guidance, and the resulting outcomes were more wonderful than I could have imagined. I also had the pattern of trying to orchestrate my life on my own which had a way of working for periods of time until a situation or event revealed how miserable I was at calling all the shots, and how futile and lonely a task it was.

Sitting on the plastic chair in the heavy heat stripped of most of the things I took for granted in the United States like my physical comfort, using my time as I chose, and the resources of transportation, communication, and entertainment, the lessons on the lack of control were clear. If the realization of my need to turn my concerns over to God had not sunk in, then a glance down at my left foot with the blister the size of a nickel and Jim's flip-flops served to remind me that this mission in this place and time had challenges I could not anticipate.

For me, this mission was high stakes. I had represented myself as qualified to open Hope and Resurrection Secondary School, friends and family were encouraging Jim and me from afar, and people had given generous donations for this endeavor. Never in my life had I stepped out into the limelight and made my faith and passions so visible to others. No

---

[3] Nye, Robert and Richard Hook, Beowulf, London: Beaver, 1985. Print.

wonder I felt anxious and sometimes downright panicked because I was afraid I would fail. I considered the shame I would feel if I could not do what I had come to do. How would I face the disappointment of others?

Re-reading what I had written in my journal, I came face to face with my ego-based fears that were about my pride and vanity. Realizing I would never succeed in even the tiniest way if I spent all my energy on protecting my ego, I prayed to forget myself and embrace whatever lay ahead. From that perspective, I believed I could go forward, blister and all, trusting that my call to this mission was real and that God was not about to abandon me to my own puny devices.

The newly acquired understanding of letting go of my fears and depending on God's grace and guidance prepared me to handle an unexpected event that otherwise would have caused great grief. There was not much to occupy us in the dusty, small town of Rumbek. A big treat was to walk the equivalent of two blocks to a cyber café to check email. One evening we headed there anticipating hearing from friends and family for their news encouraged us, and we would talk about the messages often during the following day. There were several emails, but the one we were most pleased to receive was from our son, Mark. We opened the message and sat side by side reading.

Hi Guys,

I need to first preface this email by saying that although this news will sound bad, I promise you it is not anywhere near as bad as it may seem and I have been in total control of the situation to this point

I received a call from a very upset Christine (the girl staying at the house) on Friday (3/14). She informed me that there had been a fire at the house. I was as horrified, as I'm sure you are now. Fortunately, no one was injured whatsoever. The fire started in the back-left corner of the living room next to the sliding glass door and was contained to that area. To clarify the house looks fine from any angle on the outside and it is totally structurally sound. I am SOOOOOOO sorry to give you this news! Please know that everything that can be done has been done to this point. As of now, you being here would not be necessary. We will know a lot more Monday. This situation will be OK, and I will do anything necessary to make that so. We all love you and will support you totally. Again, this is not as bad as it may seem. Love and Prayers, Mark

We could barely comprehend that there had been a fire in our Northern California house. The brief time that we had been in Africa made it seem even more impossible to believe. I scanned the message for word about our house sitter, Christine, and her three-year-old son. When I read they were unhurt, I was weak with relief because if something had happened to them in our home, I knew the depth of my anguish would be like no other. We replied to Mark and walked back to the compound where we were staying. Unanswered questions comprised our conversation.

Lying in the dark unable to sleep, I mentally inventoried my household beginning in the living room where the fire had started in faulty wiring. We had decorated the living room with our collection of American native arts and crafts which we had acquired during our forty years of married life. I recalled in vivid detail the geometric designs and the natural colors of grays and browns set against intense reds in the Navajo rugs. Each rug represented a long-ago vacation with our young sons to such places as Mesa Verde National Park and Santa Fe. I saw the shape of each basket that had been passed down to Jim from his father, and the painted, smooth surface of the pottery chosen with care. Not having any idea what had been spared in the smoke and heat, I remembered them all, and then in my imagination parted with them.

I did not experience the grief I had expected to feel, and I shed no tears lying under the holey mosquito net. Gratitude followed the relief that our house-sitter and her son were unharmed because I would have I traded all my possessions and more for their safety. I felt appreciation for Mark because writing us the news must have been difficult, and I sensed he had taken on the shock of the event and had not passed on the worst to us.

The only control that was mine was my response to this event. From the other side of the world from my home, I decided to trust God, family, friends, and the insurance company. There was grit in my decision, for during the night I prayed for God's help to move on with the business of opening the secondary school. I didn't realize at the time that the surrender of material things was part two of the lesson on giving up the illusion of control. Letting go of concerns thousands of miles away would pave the way for embracing new ideas and experiences.

After reading about my beginning weeks in Africa, do you wonder how the outcome of this mission will turn out? I wondered the same thing at the time. Nothing was going as planned, and I doubted my ability to play a key role in opening Hope and Resurrection Secondary. When remembering those first days of fear and worry, I think of the story in the Gospel of John about the disciples after the crucifixion of Jesus.

John 20:19 says: *"On the evening of that first day of the week, when the disciples were together, with the doors locked for fear of the Jewish leaders ..."* I imagine the disciples believed that the terror and grief of the last days of Jesus's life would continue. With no hope of having any control over what would happen to them, they were afraid. Their confusion and fear must have felt like a failure.

John 20: 20-22 goes on to tell: *Jesus came and stood among them and said, "Peace be with you!" As the Father has sent me, I am sending you."* And with *that he breathed on them and said, "Receive the Holy Spirit."* Jesus came to his disciples through the locked doors and exchanged their loss and fear for the astonishing gift of peace and the Holy Spirit. The rest of the story is about the disciples going boldly forth and sharing the story of Jesus with the world.

I relate to the disciples' fear because my fear of failure momentarily overshadowed my belief that I was called to be in Southern Sudan to open a school. I identify with the disciples' lack of control because I, too, couldn't call the shots about things like the house-fire thousands of miles away, or whether we had a headmaster, or if students would come to Hope and Resurrection Secondary. Like the disciples, the fears lessened when I exchanged my fear for the Holy Spirit's guidance.

Relating the chapter's theme to your life: Recall times when you were afraid, and God provided you with assurance and peace. Consider the circumstances of one of those times that stand out for you.

Matthew 19:26

CHAPTER 2

QUESTIONS AND ACTIVITIES

If you are meeting with a group, take turns relating your personal story to one another that answers the following question. If you are reading on your own, record your story in your notebook.

Relating the chapter's theme to your life: Recall times when you were afraid, and God provided you with assurance and peace. Consider the circumstances of one of those times that stand out for you—where, and when.

The theme of Chapter 2 is overcoming fear and trusting in God's presence and grace in your life. It can be challenging to acknowledge and give up pride and vanity that is often at the center of our fears. To trust God's guidance there needs to be a recognition of the things over which you have no control, followed by prayerfully giving those situations to God. The belief that God works in all things for good assures us that God's presence is with us. (Romans 8:28 - *And we know that in all things God works for the good of those who love him, who have been called according to his purpose.*)

Isaiah 12:2—*Surely God is my salvation; I will trust and not be afraid. The* L<small>ORD</small>, *the* L<small>ORD</small> *himself, is my strength and my defense he has become my salvation."*

Philippians 4:6-7—*Do not be anxious about anything, but in every situation, by prayer and petition, with thanksgiving, present your requests to God.* ⁷*And the peace of God, which transcends all understanding, will guard your hearts and your minds in Christ Jesus.*

John 20:19-22—*On the evening of that first day of the week, when the disciples were together, with the doors locked for fear of the Jewish leaders. Jesus came and stood among them and said, "Peace be with you!" As the Father has sent me, I am sending you." And with that he breathed on them and said, "Receive the Holy Spirit.*

The following questions will help you identify fears and how those fears might be overcome. During the next week, continue this activity and write in your journal to develop your ideas on fear and trust. Record your thoughts and ideas in your notebook by answering the following questions:

Question 1

Think about what made the disciples afraid, and what event caused their fears to vanish. What makes you afraid? To help you get to the heart of what makes you afraid, ask yourself the following questions:

- What dreams am I not pursuing, what opportunities am I currently passing up, and what projects or activities am I not attempting?
- Try to be specific in naming the fears such as fear of being rejected, failing or looking foolish—to name a few.
- Imagine a situation where one or more of those fears became a reality and happened.
    - Could you recover from such a thing?

- o What things could you learn from the experience?
- o In what ways would God be with you at such a time?

Question 2

Consider the advice found in the Philippians passage: *but in every situation, by prayer and petition, with thanksgiving, present your requests to God.*

- In what ways would following the advice found in Philippian's help overcome your fears?
- What changes could you make in your thoughts, prayers, and actions to more closely align them with the Philippian's passage?
- How do you include an attitude of thanksgiving in your prayers?

If you are working on your own, re-read what you have written. Sharing your thoughts from the activity and questions with a friend is a further way to explore your ideas and get feedback.

If you are working in a small group, meet back in your group and as each person is comfortable, share any thoughts and insights. End the meeting with prayer and affirmation for the insights the group brought forward.

CHAPTER 3

A Transformative Lesson—Losses and Gains

Psalm 16:8—*I keep my eyes always on the LORD. With him at my right hand, I will not be shaken.*

Mark 8:35—*For whoever wants to save their life will lose it, but whoever loses their life for me and for the gospel will save it.*

In the first days, while we eased into our new lives in Southern Sudan, I thought that the people who led our two-week missionary training program had left out some crucial information that was necessary for us to settle in and get started.

But, I soon realized that something else was going on. There were no words or explanations that our trainers could have used that would have conveyed the transformation that would take place in our heads and hearts once we were at our mission post. We had to experience it directly. On the surface, I could describe the radical adjustment that I needed to make as a lesson in flexibility and adaptability, but that does not express the depth of the changes that were required.

When we were in the United States, the job of opening and running Hope and Resurrection Secondary School for its first year seemed more about to-do lists and practical considerations than about spiritual transformation. But, I soon discovered my role in the unfamiliar environment of rural South Sudan was less about doing and more about sharing myself and responding to others. I needed to learn how to let my guard down when interacting with church and community leaders, and our students and neighbors.

Jim and I wanted to establish a positive relationship with the bishop. Our first meeting with him had been disappointing, and we hoped to reach some understanding while we were still in Rumbek waiting for the truck of supplies to arrive from Uganda. Because some things still needed to be resolved, Jim and I decided not to wait for a formal invitation but to take the initiative to visit him.

We set off to see the bishop. A steady stream of visitors was coming and going, sitting in a circle, and seeking a moment with the bishop. We entered tentatively, not sure exactly of our place. We greeted and shook the hand of each person there as we had seen others do. The bishop was not in his chair, but he reappeared to tell Jim and me that he was leaving to check the Internet, as he did weekly, and that he would be back to see us at five o'clock. We recognized that we were dismissed, not without kindness but with firmness, and that we were expected to leave. Waiting for others and for things to happen was the usual pattern of our recent days, so we took our dismissal in stride.

Since we had already ventured out into the heat, we decided to check our email as well. But, before we could do so, we were stopped by a Dinka man who communicated that we were to return to see the bishop immediately. We re-entered through the corrugated steel gate and returned to under the mango tree where the bishop was waiting for us. He sat back in a chair, and two other chairs were pulled up in front of him, facing him directly. The bishop explained that the Internet was down, and then he asked us what we wanted to discuss.

What did we want to discuss? Just about everything concerning the opening of the school, I wanted to say, but, of course, I didn't. Jim and I had identified two topics that we urgently needed to discuss with him. They were the need for a headmaster and the opening school ceremonies scheduled for March 31.

The bishop teased me about my notebook with lists and called them the ways of "kawajas"—the word for white people. When we brought up the need to find a headmaster, the Bishop looked down and fell silent. I slowed down my breathing and studied the trunk of the mango tree.

After some time, the bishop spoke in Dinka to some of the men sitting in nearby chairs, and a lively conversation ensued. The bishop explained to us that he had a man in mind, and he asked Matthew, one of the men nearby, to go and tell this person to come for an interview at ten o'clock the next morning. I was surprised and pleased that the bishop could settle this matter so easily. What had just occurred was certainly beyond Jim's and my ability to arrange.

We then moved forward to discuss the opening of the school and how best to coordinate the invitations for honored guests and arrange for the order of the speeches. The bishop seemed unhappy as we discussed this topic, but we did not understand why. The initial fits and starts of the conversation felt like it does when you dance with someone for the first time and end up stepping on each other's toes. The bishop apparently was annoyed because he had received some emails from the US that made him think that he had not been consulted in the plans as he should have been.

We negotiated this tense conversation as best we could, and it seemed like it was time to leave.

As we were about to depart, I remembered that I had brought a small picture album of photos from our November visit that I had made especially for the bishop. I pulled it from my purse.

"What is it that you have?" the bishop asked.

I answered, "A small gift for you."

This personal gift was well received, and the awkward dance between us changed. For nearly two hours, the bishop shared stories with us about his recent trip to the United States. We prayed together at the end with Jim leading the prayers. The bishop became someone we could approach because of that meeting.

The mission began in earnest when the truck with all our supplies finally arrived from Kampala. The road-weary drivers picked us up in Rumbek, and we drove the two-plus hours to the village of Atiaba and Hope and Resurrection Secondary School. For the residents of remote Atiaba, our arrival was exciting, and in minutes the vacant school compound was full of curious people like it was an old-fashioned country fair. The truck was unloaded quickly by the villagers, and all the boxes and bags piled into an empty classroom. We shook hands and met many tall, young men who told us they wanted to be students at the new school.

By now we were feeling good with all the supplies secured, the Toyota pickup truck in our possession, and the warm welcome from the residents of Atiaba. Just as we were saying goodbye and preparing to return to Rumbek for the day, the village leaders told us that the school borehole—the word for a well—located just outside the school gates was broken. Those bearing this news looked at us expectantly for the repair. Jim and I looked at each other wide-eyed. Just how did you go about getting a borehole fixed in rural Southern Sudan?

After days of inactivity, we were busy finishing business in Rumbek so that we could take up residence at the school. I met with Anthony, the man whom the Bishop had found to be headmaster of Hope and Resurrection Secondary School. I had to listen carefully to understand Anthony's African pronunciation of English, and he was not forthcoming with a great deal of information. I studied the tall, thin, neatly dressed man sitting stiffly across from me, and I wondered if we could successfully share administrative duties. We were counting on this local Dinka man to help us navigate the customs and the language, and he was our one and only candidate. After Anthony and I had parted, I realized that I had no way to contact him, I did not know where he lived, and the only date that was firm was March 31 which was the opening ceremony of the school. I had to trust that he would show up in Atiaba.

Within a few days, we finalized an order from a local business for desks, hired Anthony, and repaired the borehole. The only thing left was to meet the plane of our Ugandan teacher, Cleous, whom we had hired weeks before in Kampala to teach biology, geography, and business. Stepping off the small plane onto the dirt runway, Cleous brought the good news that the pastor in Kampala, who had agreed to continue to look for a math teacher for us, had found one. The math teacher's name was Samson, and he would be joining us in about a month.

As soon as we collected Cleous's bags, we drove out of Rumbek by way of the unpaved road which was full of potholes the size of bathtubs and kitchen sinks. From this day on, our home would be Atiaba and Hope and Resurrection Secondary. I made our first pot of beans and rice for lunch which was not very tasty, but Jim and Cleous ate heartily. Cleous assured me that the leftover beans and rice could sit for the next six hours with no refrigeration and reheated for supper. Would we die our first week of food poisoning? Cleous, who grew up in a small village in Uganda, thought that we would not.

We ate the leftover beans and rice by kerosene lantern light that evening. We sat outside after supper in our brand new plastic chairs which are a staple in Southern Sudan. Jim and Cleous each tried the solar bag shower devised by hanging the shower bag from a tree branch and creating privacy by hanging an orange tarp from a suspended framework. Leftover building bricks made the floor of the improvised shower.

"I will shower tomorrow in the daylight when I can see what I am doing," I told Jim. I made my first visit to the latrine. The small latrine building had two separate stalls, each with a square hole in the concrete floor which you had to squat over. Although I was used to camping, the idea of that square hole for the next ten months was daunting.

In the inky, black sky with no light pollution, the Milky Way seemed only an arm's length away. Noises from the village gradually lessened until it was quiet. I thought about the last week and felt grateful for our safety, the repaired borehole, Cleous's arrival, and that we were in the good favor of our neighbors.

When we finally crawled into bed that first night and arranged the mosquito netting around us, neither Jim nor I could sleep immediately. Many months later, Jim told me that he had wondered what we had gotten ourselves into as he fell asleep in the classroom-turned-into-a-bedroom with only a bent nail to secure the screen door shut. On my side of the bed, I was thinking in terms of specifics as opposed to Jim's generalities. I was deciding that I could not spend the next ten months not showering and avoiding using the latrine. I would have to get used to all these things. As we fell asleep, the hyenas across the road in the forest began to moan in their low, tortured-sounding way of communicating with one another.

\#

People of the Dinka tribe are tall, and their body shape is very slim. Their skin is the beautiful dark color of bittersweet chocolate, and their curly hair is kept very short. Did God make them exactly right for the hot climate? I knew I wasn't made for it. I felt short and chalky white, my skin got red blotches in the sun, and my straight hair hung limply.

Jim and I never had the luxury of just blending into a crowd; our white skin made us objects of curiosity. It was odd to know that you were closely watched. Neighbors would come to the school for a visit and tell us what we had done that day. They would say things like, "Mary washed clothes and James drove to the clinic in Akot." We would smile and say "Yes, that is what we did."

Since I was learning how to manage my new lifestyle—how to do laundry in a plastic tub and hang my clothes to dry on fences and bushes, cook on a two-burner propane stove, store food with no refrigeration, wash dishes with no running water, and handle personal grooming without the benefit of things like a hair dryer—I would have preferred a bit more privacy while figuring it out. But the sincere overtures of friendship made up for the sense that I was living in a fishbowl.

I was soon used to the external things in my environment, but the internal landscape of my thoughts and sense of comfort with others and myself took longer. There was a gap between how I defined myself in the context of my life in the United States and how my new neighbors saw me. My Sudanese neighbors would not understand the pride I took in my master's degree in education, or that I had been Teacher of the Year in the school district where I taught. The enjoyment that I get from using the family silver for dinner guests, as well as fresh flowers and candles, would make no sense to those who cooked over an open fire and did not use utensils to eat. My neighbors walked miles to the marketplace or to take care of their herds of goats and cattle, so my accomplishment of hiking the Grand Canyon would not be a big deal to them. The vast gulf between my life in the US and the lives of my Atiaba neighbors stripped me of the usual things that created my identity.

Without the things that I was used to in the US which provided entertainment and distractions, I had plenty of time to ponder how to make connections with my neighbors. Some of the things that put me in good standing with them were that I remembered people's names, greeted them with the traditional handshake, and played games with the village children. My neighbors appreciated that I waited patiently for my turn with the other women to pump water from the well. They liked the respect I showed the students who were registering for school.

Because my Dinka neighbors did not understand the things I valued that were a part of my US identity, I discovered a plainer, simpler version of myself. Had I worn my degrees and accomplishments like pieces of jewelry to adorn myself? Had I used my accolades to impress and even to hide behind to disguise my lack of confidence? Had I become so used to the dolled-up image that I had fashioned for myself that I undervalued the plain and basic offering of compassion and respect which resided deep in my being?

In response to these questions, I imagined a revised version of my self-image in the form of a weaving. The warp or vertical threads which gave strength and structure were made up of my faith in God, my belief in human potential, my respect for cultural differences, my joy in teaching, and my desire for justice for all. The weft threads which created the pattern and ran horizontally were the circumstances of my life and included education, experiences, and abilities. I then understood that I needed to incorporate the things of my new life in Southern Sudan into the pattern if my days were to have meaning and purpose. The weaving image reconnected me to why I had come to Southern Sudan and what I was offering, imperfections and all. This way of thinking made vulnerability— the honest sharing of myself—no longer so intimidating.

During my first weeks at Hope and Resurrection Secondary, I had the perfect opportunity to put into practice the revised version of myself.

Instead of being overly anxious about the correct thing to do, I reacted in the way I thought was best. It happened one afternoon in mid-April when we had been living at the school for less than a month, and Hope and Resurrection Secondary had not started yet.

Six women visited us. They had walked over an hour to get to the school to ask if we would hire them to cook and clean. I was dismayed because we did not have the work or budget to employ six women. It was also impractical to hire people who lived so far from the school. We brought out the plastic chairs and put them in the shade of the big mahogany tree. Through the translator who had accompanied the women, I gently explained that we did not have jobs.

The six were all middle-aged and most likely had their children almost raised since motherhood began at an early age. They wore brightly colored, mismatched skirts and tops, and some had long rectangular pieces of chiffon tied under one arm and brought over the opposite shoulder, a look that was considered high fashion. It was evident that they came prepared to impress, and they succeeded. Sitting with them in the circle, they captured my admiration for their initiative to visit the school and for their willingness to take any job, even one so far from home.

I knew from observing women in the village that they worked very hard taking care of household tasks and their children and that society regarded their role as serving others. These six women inspired me to want to do something for them. I turned to the young man who was their translator. "Please ask them if they would like a cup of tea." He seemed to regard my offer of tea to these women as inappropriate because he just sat there and did not do as I had asked. Calmly but firmly, I asked him again to inquire if the ladies wanted tea. After a pause, he relayed my message, and I was rewarded by six smiles.

I went into my makeshift kitchen which was an empty classroom furnished with a table, chairs, and shelves for the dishware and pots we had bought in Kampala, and a small two burner propane stove. If I had been their guest, they would have had to heat the water over an open fire or a smoky charcoal cooker. When the hot tea was in cups, I arranged it on my cutting board like a tray and went outside to serve them. I added our canister of sugar because I knew that sugar was a treat. We sat in a quiet circle, sipping and smiling. I was learning not to be uneasy when there was no conversation since I could not say much in Dinka. It was good not to talk but to just sit under the tree with these ladies. After tea, they left to walk over an hour back home, and I tucked the tea party memory away.

A week later in the early afternoon, I went to the borehole just outside the school's gate to get water in a jerry can for washing the lunch dishes. A woman arrived at the well and greeted me, and I recognized her as one of the six from the week before. She came back into the school compound with me and talked in Dinka to Anthony. Anthony explained that this woman had walked the hour from her village to bring me mangoes and that the mangoes were a thank you for treating her and her friends in such a kindly fashion. I knew how to say thank you in Dinka and did so with enthusiasm.

The tea party was a benchmark event for me because in deciding to serve the six women, I had trusted myself. I offered them the hospitality that I thought was right instead of worrying if I was following the proper custom. Hosting the impromptu tea party reassured me that being myself was going to be enough and that God was guiding my decisions. I did not have to "play it safe."

#

In the discernment process of becoming a missionary, I had read and thought a great deal about vocation. I believe that my vocation is to be a teacher based on the joy it gives me and the effectiveness I have with my students. But, my confidence in the American educational way of doing things did not prepare me to encounter a very different system of instruction in Africa.

My dilemma was deciding how to use the authority given to me by the Hope for Humanity organization. The reality was that American educational best practices did not dovetail neatly into the educational structure that the Dinka headmaster and Ugandan teachers understood. Jim and I asked ourselves if we had any right to impose our way of doing things on the African staff, especially because we would be at the school for only one or two school years.

If I asked myself the question that way, then, of course, the answer was no. If there were an adjustment, then the missionaries would make it—Jim and me—not the African staff. As mature as that conclusion sounds, the process of reaching it caused me to have many moments of being unsure about my teaching capabilities which in the past had been my most significant source of confidence and pride.

The students in Southern Sudan learn by taking copious notes based on what is written on the blackboard and memorizing things by repeating them over and over. The American way usually is to read the text with the students, make sense of the meaning through discussion and examples, and then take brief, concise notes. Our way of instruction made the students anxious, and they complained to Anthony. Jim and I tried ways to soften our American approach but keep the essence of critical thinking and problem-solving.

Jim worked with the students in the physics class to encourage a natural curiosity and to provide them with an alternative to their usual practice of memorizing formulas without understanding them. He added to our limited lab supplies by taking small empty tomato paste cans and filling them up with wet concrete from a building site to become weights for hands-on learning aids about mass. Gradually, students began to enjoy the opportunities for experimentation and the sense of discovery that Jim provided for them.

In my English classes, all seemed to be going well until about four weeks into the school year. The students were beginning to chat among themselves and work on other class notes, and they were not engaging wholeheartedly in their lessons. Was it because they were older and had a break in school attendance after primary school? Was attending secondary school full time challenging them more than I had initially realized?

I modified their English lessons and activities over the next few weeks, but the students' marginal participation remained the same. As a result, I began questioning myself and my ability to be the teacher that the students needed. I was deeply troubled by this thought, for what would it mean to the success of the students and the school if I was the wrong person for this time and place?

The feelings this situation elicited were similar to the ones I experienced during my first year of teaching eighth-grade classes in a large California middle school. Most of the student population had been made up of teens from at-risk or non-English speaking homes. I was a brand-new teacher facing kids who often chose to act out and not cooperate due to the challenging circumstances of their lives. Out of concern and frustration, one day I made a speech, and the essence of it was that I did not care if the students liked me because teaching was not a popularity contest, but I did care that they were prepared to succeed in high school English class next year. Thirty-five teens stared back at me, and for several seconds the room was quiet. Then, from the back of the room, a student named Jolene said, "But we do like you, Mrs. Higbee," and the other students nodded in agreement. Jolene's response challenged me to engage the students in a meaningful dialogue about the situation, rather than scolding them.

The lesson that I learned from this early experience in my teaching career was how important honesty is in the classroom for achieving meaningful results and for rising above any obstacles that present themselves. But, to exercise honesty with my Sudanese students held a risk. What would I do if the discussion went wrong? Would the students' answer be that I had failed at being their teacher in ways I did not culturally understand?

Each day my concern grew, and finally, on a Friday morning, I faced the students and said something like this: "How you have been acting in this class feels disrespectful to me. There must be a problem, and I would like you to be truthful with me. Is it because I am white, or because I am a woman, or because I am an American, or is it all three reasons? I need to know because if I am not the right teacher for you, then we need to do something about it." My heart was pounding, as I waited for their response. It felt as if I were naked, but what I had really exposed was my desire to be the teacher they needed and my fear that I wasn't.

In response, the students murmured to one another and looked at me wide-eyed. "Oh no, Madame Mary, it is not any of those things. What you say is not true." Their surprise at my question seemed sincere, and it took a moment for me to regain composure from the flood of emotions that welled up in me. My question to them set in motion a discussion about the challenges of secondary school, my goals for them in English class, and how I planned to move forward with them if I had their cooperation. I do not think anyone had ever discussed goals and strategies in a way that made the students partners in their learning, and they caught my enthusiasm and agreed to work on this.

Our talk cleared the air and paved the way for academic progress and some fun with literature and writing. I presented the kinds of lessons I knew worked with learners of English as a second language. My immigrant students in the US had appeared to know English when interacting with their peers, but they lacked the academic vocabulary necessary to succeed in school. The Hope and Resurrection students also needed words and more words. I set out to give them as many new words each day as I could.

After reading a short story in the English book, I asked the students to tell me which character they admired the most and why. Before they could answer this question, though, I had to explain what the word "admire" meant. The room fell silent, and the students began to look for the correct answer in the pages of the story. A student said, "Mary, this is so hard. I do not see the answer."

"The answer is not in the book. The answer is what you think about the characters, and there can be more than one correct answer," I told them. I had to coax the students to trust their thinking. Their past school experiences had emphasized that there was one correct answer, and the students were not encouraged to do any independent thinking. Reading literature together provided opportunities for students to begin claiming the worth of their ideas.

In hindsight, I believe that my being a woman was the foundational cause of their negative behavior in those first weeks of school because I was nothing like their mothers, sisters, and in some cases, wives. Even the three female students did not know how to interpret the new model that I represented. I don't think that the students were aware of the source of their attitude and actions because it was deeply rooted in their culture and traditions. My instruction helped them to be better readers and writers, but I think the most valuable lesson came from my being myself and modeling independence and professional competence in a place that had not yet come to view women as having those traits.

#

In early May, our Toyota truck's rear leaf spring broke. Fortunately, Jim was able to get the truck to a neighboring missionary's compound

49

where they maintained vehicles. We handed over five hundred dollars to a Ugandan friend who was going on a buying trip to Uganda and was willing to buy the part we needed.

There were only two vehicles in area, and our Toyota truck was one of them. The truck represented freedom of mobility and access to resources that were not nearby such as a marketplace, a source of fuel, banking services, and an Internet connection. The people of Atiaba and the students of the school also depended on us to transport the sick and injured to the medical clinic six miles away and for rides into Rumbek.

Not having transportation posed problems constantly, and we often had no idea how they would be solved. We walked or biked the twelve miles round-trip to check emails, but we had no way to get to Rumbek to the bank for money to pay for supplies and the payroll for the crew from Kenya that was building the teachers' quarters within the school compound.

By this time, I believed I had fully adjusted to life in Atiaba and lived like my neighbors, but the loss of transportation revealed that I had been kidding myself. Having transportation provided freedom for me that had never been the experience of the students or people of Atiaba. I wrote this account in my journal:

> Just like everyone else, we wait for a ride that might be available in the next five minutes, five days, or never. We put the word out that we need to get to the bank, and then we wait. If a ride does not materialize, we will need to decide what to do because the contractor needs to pay for supplies. We have not formed Plan B yet.
>
> Then, in the middle of a busy Tuesday morning, a car pulls into the school compound. The driver has come from the medical clinic six miles down the road and is headed to Rumbek. Jim runs

for the bank records and his passport and gratefully squeezes into the already full car.

Is this Plan A or B? Actually, it is neither. As we are discovering, Africans live with a sense of expectation while making the best of the situation, so that it hardly seems like they are waiting, and the grace of God is given the credit when something good happens.

Anyone who knows my aptitude for planning and scheduling must realize how often I have had to practice this lesson of letting go. I have not mastered it yet, I am sure, but I am glad that there is some measurable progress in just flowing with what the day brings.

#

On a Friday morning, when the school was well underway, the head teacher of a large primary school paid a visit and invited the students and staff to attend a celebration ceremony the next day. The Toyota truck was still broken, and a local official with a vehicle had room for only one more person. Jim, Cleous, Samson, and Anthony unanimously voted that I should go. I appreciated being the one to represent the school because I did not always have the opportunities that the men had to be away from the school compound due to the safety concerns inherent in being a woman in Southern Sudan.

I had not taken many clothes to Southern Sudan, so, for this special occasion, I chose my favorite denim skirt and a pink knit shirt from the things hanging on a makeshift clothes rod that Jim had designed. As I dressed, I remembered the day I bought the skirt at Macy's Labor Day sales, and how I had wandered through attractive, bright aisles with a myriad of enticing choices before deciding to buy this skirt. Getting dressed in the classroom that was my bedroom, the denim skirt seemed to represent to me some incredible feat of time travel from one faraway lifestyle in California to this life in a rural village in Southern Sudan. I smiled to myself as I realized that I was now firmly planted in Southern Sudan and very present to the people and place.

The ceremony was outside in the primary schoolyard, and as one of the honored guests, I sat in the front where I listened to hours of speeches in Dinka as the ceremony proceeded. The highlight was four hundred primary students singing and marching with practiced precision around and around the schoolyard. The school uniforms that the students wore were often ragged, and their shoes were either hand-me-down scuffed leather ones or flip-flops, but the combination of their high voices singing songs of welcome and being in perfect step with one another was an inspiring sight.

Many Hope and Resurrection students had come to the ceremony since they were former students of this primary school. They had all worn their Hope and Resurrection gray t-shirts and sat together with an air of importance now that they were in secondary school. I looked at them with pride and affection for they embodied my belief that education empowers people to create a better future for themselves, and they were the reason I was in Southern Sudan.

After the ceremony, a student named Mabor came and sat with me. At age 34, Mabor was one of our oldest students and a husband and father of two. He was a huge, strong man who crammed himself into a school desk every day to learn. Mabor said to me, "The people ask us who is that white woman, and we say you are our teacher. And we are very proud."

The news that Mabor and the other students were proud to claim me as their teacher filled me with joy. The lump of emotion in my throat was from my sense of awe at how extraordinary it was to be a headmistress and teacher in Southern Sudan and to be sitting in a red dirt schoolyard with Mabor at that very moment in time. I had already decided that my most compelling qualification to be deputy headmistress was that I had been the one who had said "yes" to this mission, rather than any of my professional credentials. I certainly did not have all the answers, but Mabor's affirmation assured me that having all the answers was not what they expected of me.

I had never made the connection between vulnerability and humility. When I was open to sharing myself and accepting others, my students and neighbors and I regarded one another with trust and good humor. Being vulnerable with each other naturally elicited a sense of humility, but this humility was different from any I had experienced before. Instead of feelings of self-effacement and being less worthy or important in comparison to others, I felt the kind of humility that recognizes and appreciates others. As my regard for those around me was elevated, I felt increasingly connected to others. I felt a sense of peace and belonging that I hadn't felt before, and I wore this feeling like a lovely, new garment.

I measured my losses in all the ways my South Sudanese life was inconvenient and hard compared to of my Western lifestyle. I measured the gains by the positive connection that I was making in my relationships with my students and neighbors. The gains outweighed the losses. The transformation in my head and heart is evident in a blog post:

> What is most important is that we are finding our place in the community. The word community in the United States often designates a physical locale, but here it means a complex structure of relationships and a system for collective decision making. We are learning how things are done and taking a role in participating. The paramount chief visited today and invited us to go to church tomorrow which is held under a tree in the village. We can drive seven miles and worship in a stone church in another village, but the chief made it clear he hoped we would be a part of the Atiaba

tree church. After he left, I wondered if the invitation was more than just for church but was an invitation to belong in a larger sense. So, it seems that the biggest challenges have been our dearest gains, and we have increasingly become able to relax and enjoy the people in this community. We are making our way through situations without the cultural clues that we take for granted when we are at home in the United States.

Relating the chapter's theme to your life: Recall a time when you had to change the way you were used to doing something or an idea that no longer fit with your life circumstances. In making the change, what did you lose and what did you gain?

Matthew 19:26

CHAPTER 3

QUESTIONS AND ACTIVITIES

If you are meeting with a group, take turns relating your personal story to one another that answers the following question. If you are reading on your own, record your story in your notebook.

Relating the chapter's theme to your life: Recall a time when you had to change the way you were used to doing something or an idea that no longer fit with your life circumstances. In making the change, what did you lose and what did you gain?

Chapter 3 recounts the spiritual transformation that took place when I put aside some of the things from my life in the United States that had made me feel important. In the place of titles, degrees, and awards that kept me focused on myself, I looked outward to the needs of my neighbors and students. The transfer of my attention away from myself to others prompted an attitude of compassion. The mission required that I adapt to an educational system that was not American and take up my role as headmistress not knowing the social customs or expectations. These personal adaptations were necessary so that I could embrace the new ideas and responsibilities. It was at the farthest edge of my comfort zone that I found a deeper trust in God and courage to step into each day.

The slower pace of life in Southern Sudan allowed me to notice answered prayers, and I often paused to feel gratitude for things which at first seemed insignificant like a glimpse of a bright yellow bird in the forest or the shy smile of a child. I adopted the image of a weaving for my new life in Southern Sudan. The weaving image made me mindful of the daily practices and ways of thinking that provided balance and support for my spiritual life in a place so far away from home.

Psalm 16:8—*I keep my eyes always on the LORD. With him at my right hand, I will not be shaken.*

Mark 8:35—*For whoever wants to save their life will lose it, but whoever loses their life for me and for the gospel will save it.*

The verse in Mark prescribes the challenging work of letting go of our carefully constructed façades of self-importance. In doing so, we discover the person we are meant to be and the God-given gifts we possess. Worries and anxiety lessen because we focus less on what other people think and become free to befriend the people whom we choose and pursue the work that gives us purpose. When we cease to see life as a competition, we can be vulnerable and open to others.

Another outcome of adjusting our ego-based sense of self and finding who we are as a beloved child of God is that we become mindful of the sustaining patterns woven through our daily routines and relationships with others. Choosing practices that make us aware of God's presence is one way we mature in knowing ourselves and growing in our faith and commitment to God. Psalm 16:8 assures us that though we experience many changes throughout our life, God will hold us steady.

The following activity guides you to review the things that you are doing that support your spiritual and emotional well-being. Record your responses in your journal.

Part 1

An appraisal of how your life reflects your values and beliefs helps you recognize the daily practices that are sustaining your spiritual journey. Consider how you integrate prayer, study, work, recreation, service to others, self-care, and hospitality into your busy life. There are no right or wrong responses to the following questions, and your answers will provide awareness of your current spiritual landscape. Answer the questions with positive statements about what you are doing in each area and avoid critiquing what you write.

- Prayer and worship - In what ways do you seek God's presence and guidance?

- Study – How do you increase your knowledge of God?

- Self-care and recreation - How do you re-energize and renew? What settings give you joy and with whom do you like to share them? In what ways do you take care of yourself?

- Work – How do you find meaning in your work? The word "work" can be what you do at a job, volunteering or the work you do to maintain your home and take care of family and friends

- Hospitality and service to others - How do you share hospitality with others? What do you do to serve others? Service and hospitality can occur in our homes, churches, and local organizations—wherever you are willing to be of service to others?

Part 2

Your answers from Part 1 represent the things in your life right now that promote spiritual growth and reflect your intentional seeking of the Holy Spirit. By writing them down, you have become more mindful of your practices.

- What practices and activities seem to fit in more than one category?
- Review your answers and consider what you might add in the future to what you are already doing. Where would you like to put your attention, in what areas do you desire to grow, and how will you achieve a better balance between the different areas of your daily life? Add your thoughts on these questions in your notebook.
- What practices and activities are not helping you sustain a balance of mind, body, and spirit? If you acted on the words of Mark 8:35 *For whoever wants to save their life will lose it, but whoever loses their life for me and for the gospel will save it* what attitudes, habits, and ways of thinking would you alter or abandon to bring you closer to God?

If you are working on your own, re-read what you have written. Sharing your thoughts from the activity and questions with a friend is a further way to explore your ideas and get feedback.

If you are working in a small group, meet back in your group and as each person is comfortable, share any thoughts and insights. End the meeting with prayer and affirmation for the insights the group brought forward.

During the week continue to think about how your daily routine supports your spiritual growth and record any new thoughts in your journal.

Matthew 19:26

LIVING INTO GOD'S MISSION

CHAPTER 4

Community—The Give and Take of Acceptance and Caring

Ecclesiastes 4:9-10—*Two are better than one, because they have a good return for their labor: If either of them falls down, one can help the other up.*

Hebrews 10:24-25—*And let us consider how we may spur one another on toward love and honorable deeds, not giving up meeting together, as some are in the habit of doing, but encouraging one another—and all the more as you see the Day approaching.*

Before we went to Southern Sudan, we met a couple who had served as missionaries in El Salvador, a place which is considered very violent. The story they shared with us was about meeting the El Salvadoran bishop for whom they were going to work. He told them he could not keep them safe.

They were shocked and frightened that he offered no hope for their protection. But then the bishop added, "I can't keep you safe, but those whom you will serve and love, and who will love you in return will keep you safe."

We remembered the couple's story as we settled into our life at Hope and Resurrection Secondary. We had come to stand with the community of Atiaba by opening the secondary school but for us to accomplish that, people had to stand by us, too. Jim and I knew from past experiences that an individual acting alone often has less of an impact than when a group works together towards a common goal. Most often it takes a team of people, each offering their unique gifts to the cause or project. The African proverb that says that it takes a village to raise a child has universal applications to just about everything in life.

It only took a day to realize our neighbors were not shy about becoming our friends. Dinka people are masters at being fully present to others. According to their cultural norms, you would never pass anyone without both a greeting and an inquiry as to his or her health. You always shake hands and are never too hurried to honor this tradition. A constant trickle of people passed through the gates of the school compound to greet Jim and me as we settled into living there.

On day two of our moving and settling in, a delegation of chiefs and leaders came to the school and said to Jim, "You will take us to Karich," which was a village about five miles up the road. Jim was taken back by their demand, rather than a request. The delegation wanted a ride to Karich immediately, so Jim quickly had to decide how to respond. Jim nodded yes, and they piled into the Toyota with the most important among them sitting inside the cab, and the others bouncing along in the bed of the truck.

When Jim returned to the school, he told me he had taken the men to attend a gathering of leaders from all the neighboring villages. He grinned as he described their obvious pleasure in arriving in one of the few vehicles in the area, much like the red-carpet treatment for movie stars in limousines. Jim and I talked about our concern that the men had been demanding and recalled the advice we had received about being careful in sharing resources so that relationships stayed healthy. Despite all of this, however, Jim believed that his gut reaction to take them had prompted him to make the correct decision.

It did not take long for us to realize that the Dinka language does not have a word for "please." As a result, our neighbors had not known about the subtly of using "please" to accompany a request, especially given that English was their second language. Once we realized that, we saw that the men's communication was not the aggressive demand it had seemed to be but just their cultural misunderstanding of American etiquette and the unspoken rules for making polite requests. When Jim tells this story, he concludes by saying what a good decision it was to take the men because when he needed their help later, they were glad to pitch in, reminding him of the day he had driven them to Karich.

#

It took almost a month before we could get down to the business of registering students for the first class to be admitted to the school. I wrote in a blog post:

> The student body is shaping up with the oldest student being 37. For Jim and me, a central part of the mission is to provide a second chance opportunity for these older students who urgently desire an education. After graduating from primary 8 (eighth grade), most of these students had no opportunity for further schooling or paid employment and, as a result, became unpaid pastors or primary teachers, teaching children under a big tree with a blackboard as

their only teaching aid. Our future students are intelligent, mature, polite, and very likable.

Also, there is another big group of students who are in their twenties and started primary school when they were older. They are eager and full of high spirits and greet us with enthusiastic handshakes and big smiles.

Then there are our three young women in their late teens. In the tradition of this culture, it is unusual that they are not already married and that their fathers value education enough to allow them to go to secondary school. Many Dinka women are illiterate. There is much work to do each day in the home, and girls are trained to do these household tasks rather than go to school. Our female students are named Angelina, Deborah, and Mary.

On the first official day of school, Anthony, Cleous, Jim and I, and Samson, who had recently arrived from Uganda, met the students in a classroom. Anthony explained the school rules, and we each presented a short lesson. I felt the excitement of the usual first-day-of-school nervousness. I wore my church skirt and top because I wanted to look my best. I concentrated on slowing down my speech so the students could understand me and strained to comprehend their African pronunciation of English. I shared about the day in this blog post:

Back in the saddle again – How I enjoyed being in front of students again. We all gave a short lesson, and it was great to be thinking like an educator and have the interaction with the students. Jim is teaching physics because it was what was left. He doesn't even want to calculate how many years ago that he had a college physics class. I think that he will do a good job, and I predict that he will find it satisfying. I had the last lesson of the day, and as I said goodbye to the students and wished them well, they requested that I close in prayer. As an American public-school teacher who always needed to be aware of the separation of church and state, I found this to be an amazing moment and gladly complied with their wish.

It was not until June 21 that I could write:

Drum roll, please – The government exit exam for eighth graders are marked, and the list of results available. Jim picked the list up today. Wow! We can now determine the second half of the freshman class in a fair, unbiased way. We will need to be creative, developing ways to help this group of newly admitted students to catch-up with the first half of the freshman class. Finally, the school's first year is underway.

With the second half of the freshman class enrolled, Hope and Resurrection Secondary had a total of sixty freshmen. The plan was to add a class level each year, so in four years there would be all four levels from freshmen to seniors at the school.

#

Jim has always been better at hanging out than I am, and this facilitated warm relationships with many of our students. The school day was out around four in the afternoon, but those who lived just a few minutes away in the village often came back around five to borrow a textbook and to read in a classroom until dark, as well as on Saturday and Sunday. As a result, one of us teachers had to be in the school office to check textbooks in and out. Jim would often volunteer for this task, and a group of students usually joined him in the office, asking him questions about everything under the sun. The give and take with the students became one part of the job that Jim enjoyed the most.

One of the students' favorite topics was possible careers, prompted by information in the first chapter of the physics textbook that discussed the types of jobs people could have that required a knowledge of physics. Initially, the class discussions that Jim led on the topic of careers were not that promising because the students did not know what a career was and could not relate to the examples given in the textbook. As Jim worked to make the physics labs relevant to real life, some of the students began to have an interest in the kinds of things that are related to physics. Jim and the students engaged in earnest discussions about what engineers did, and Jim told stories about designing bridges, roads, and airplanes. Often the students had questions about which universities would be best to attend if they wanted to become an engineer, and Jim became the weaver of dreams that reached far beyond the small village of Atiaba.

One evening, when it was getting dark, and I had supper almost ready, Jim and some students stood talking at the compound gate. Jim finally broke away and came in, and I asked him what they had been discussing. "I said 'buenas noches' as the students were leaving, and it took ten more minutes to answer their questions about Spanish, and then they wanted to know other Spanish words." Buenas noches became a familiar farewell around the school.

#

I wanted my friends and family at home to know more about the people who were a part of our daily lives and who increasingly stood with us. I shared my observations of my neighbors in a blog post.

Dinka women – The well is just outside the school gate. I love to go to the well because I can interact with the women and children there. The men come into the school compound to greet us and visit, but the women rarely come to school, so I need to place myself where they are. The well is the perfect place.

65

The women do not know English, but I know some things to say in Dinka. They were at first surprised to see me fetch water, white skin and all, but now my joining with them pumping water has become a bond between us. When it is my turn to pump water into my jerry can—which by the way is an incredible way to reduce underarm flab—they laugh and joke with me. There are many styles of pumping, including jumping up and down. I try them all. Going to the well is a social activity, and women often go together, a great escape, I imagine, from their tukuls (round thatched-roof huts). When they have filled their jerry cans, one woman helps another to pick up her full jerry can and hoist it up on her head where she has placed a coiled rag of fabric to create a flat area for the can. The second woman is left to struggle alone to get her can up to her head because her partner can't help because she already has a jerry can of water balanced on her head. At this point, I add my help. I pick up the jerry can, and with great effort hoist it up for her as high as I can get it. No matter how often I help, I am amazed at the weight of that big can of water. "Mary, Mary," they yell and wave goodbye and glide gracefully off with perfect posture, the heavy jerry cans on their heads. They remind me of Paris runway models.

Fashion – I am ever fascinated with what the women wear. Here I am with my drip-dry-wicking-fabric-beige-go-with-anything-skirt like a drab little bird, while they are decked out like magnificent parrots. There are no color rules for them, except brightness is the best, and no concern with mixing stripes and prints. There is no money for women to buy clothes, and even if they had money, there are very few choices. Their wardrobes come from donation boxes sent from around the world and passed out by pastors in local churches. What interests me is the way the women put the hand-me-downs together. The women favor delicate fabric and silky things which doesn't seem to go with their environment of dirt floor tukuls, charcoal cooking fires, mud, dust, and much hard work, but the contrast of the clothes they like to wear and their environments makes them look especially elegant. They also like to tie a length of fabric on one shoulder and drape it under the other arm with the fabric falling around them like a one-armed jumper. This fabric might be a printed bed sheet or a piece of chiffon. Sometimes they wear big prints styled in traditional African ways. Hot pink, red, royal blue, and bright yellow dazzle the eye. Hair is kept very short because of the heat and often covered with a scarf of some kind. The women wear flip-flops for footwear which are often falling apart, and they sometimes do not wear a top in their family compounds. Not wearing a top seems to be such a practical solution to the heat and the challenges of laundry, and people in Africa are wonderfully comfortable with their bodies. The sum of all of this is that they look quite beautiful in their unique way.

Children – They are beloved, and parenthood is a serious matter. Children run naked until about five or six, and babies, who are incredibly beautiful, never wear diapers. Big families are the norm. The most natural thing in the world here is for siblings to take care of their younger siblings as a matter of course. These big brothers and sisters, who are often not more than seven or eight, carry wee ones around on their hips as they go about their day. The little ones adore and depend on their older sibling and are so comfortable that they are often seen napping in the arms of their brothers or sisters. I have never seen the older siblings tease or neglect their duty or seem to resent their assignment. In the West, we are reluctant to impose such long-term babysitting chores on our older children but doing so is survival for the mother, who has much to do for her family every day and needs the help of all her children. There are no toys, not one. The children play in groups with whatever there is—mud puddles, sticks, dirt, rocks—and they don't appear ever to be bored. The little ones like it when we "kawajas," white people, wave at them. When they spot us, they sing a chorus of "hellohellohellohello" in one continuous, joyful word that never fails to make me smile.

Boys by eight or so wear big shirts and nothing else. They are usually barefoot, and the big shirt falls off one shoulder because of their skinny bodies underneath. The boys' vigorous play and work leave their clothes torn and stained. They roam around together, seeming to have the best possible guy-type childhood in the bush, herding cattle, and swimming in the river. Girls wear dresses, and some are quite fancy, especially for going to church. These dresses most likely come from donations from first world countries. Judging by the holes and ragged lace, they are handed down through many girls. These too big dresses are rarely buttoned, and they ignore the sashes that stream by their sides rather than being tied in a bow in the back. The girls have their hair very short—almost not there—which make their features more noticeable. When they greet me in their torn dresses with their big brown eyes, high cheekbones, and broad smiles, I think of them as tattered princesses. Without mirrors, they are unaware how lovely they look.

Men – Men operate in their own society, but as a white female from the United States, I am included in their conversations. While women are at home with their children and in the company of other females, men meet for philosophical discussions in the marketplace. They appear to keep no specific hours and come and go as they wish. The problem of underemployment, as well as unemployment, is widespread here and keeping cattle or cultivating garden plots do not take all the men's time. Tasks for the family welfare are gender-specific, and men are ridiculed, for example, if they are caught preparing food. In conversations with men, I found them to be very proud of their wives and children, and they feel a responsibility to take care of them. Coming from our Western culture, Jim and I must be cautious not to project our world values and beliefs about gender onto them. Reserving judgment and just observing seems to be our best option here.

Living in a National Geographic Picture - When I see the sunset filtered through the leaves of towering mahogany trees or watch people thatch the roofs of their tukuls for the rainy season, or see teenage boys herding large humpback bulls down the dirt road, I feel like I have stepped into an issue of a National Geographic magazine. I know that I am soaking up sights that I will always remember vividly. Jim and I are also aware that in a few more decades, the scenes that we are witnessing will differ significantly from the ones that we see now. We are watching a society in transition as the agrarian way of life is being challenged by the need for jobs, goods, services, and roads. As charming as the simple life is, the challenges of clean water, education, infant mortality, and a life expectancy of 47 are daunting. The longer we are here, the more aware we are becoming of how difficult things can be for people who live in this part of the world.

#

Having a correct understanding and interpretation of what we observed in Southern Sudan was critical. If we had misunderstood the Dinka customs, we might have easily had an Alice-in-Wonderland type of

69

misadventure with great possibilities for confusion. We had to be vigilant in keeping an open mind. Our mission in Southern Sudan was not to critique the Dinka society but instead to learn how our hosts saw the world.

We had daily opportunities to watch family life because the school was located just at the edge of the village. The marriage custom of a man having more than one wife was immediately apparent to us. If a Dinka man is rich, he is likely to have two or three wives. To obtain a bride, a man needs to pay a negotiated bride price of cattle to her family. The family of the bride is made rich by acquiring many cows through the marriage of their daughter. Men often do not marry until they are in their thirties because it takes many years, along with the help of their families, to obtain enough cows to win a bride. Girls, whose fathers do not permit them to go to school, are likely to be married at 16 and be mothers at 17. Some fathers give their daughters a choice of a future husband but that is not always the case. Increasingly, Christian men choose to have only one wife.

Jim and I attended a ceremony for the inspection of the cows offered by a potential groom to the family of the young woman he wished to marry. We drove far into the bush to a compound that was lively with women cooking and men discussing politics and crops. While all this activity was going on, the bride's family inspected the cows being offered by the potential groom. This situation became even more of a drama when word came that a rival suitor was coming with his cows to offer. Dinka cows are skinny, silvery gray with brown spots, and have a humped back and Texas-style horns. To someone like me who knows nothing about farming, the skinny cows seemed hardly worth the fuss, but the bride's family looked over each of the one hundred cows with care.

The assistant Episcopal bishop gave Jim and me Dinka cow names. At first, I wondered if it was a joke to be given a cow name, but I learned that it is not unusual. Jim's name is Mabor which means white bull, and my name is Amare which means a cow with little brown freckle-like spots.

The assistant bishop who bestowed these names on us went to a lot of trouble to find a freckled cow to show me so that I could fully appreciate the meaning of my Dinka name.

I was asked by one of our male students how many children Jim and I had, and I answered that we had two sons. The person asking the question regarded us with curiosity. He wondered what tragic events had caused us to have only two children which seemed sad to him because Dinka families have as many children as possible. The student shook his head at my answer and told me, "If I pay one hundred cows for a bride, she will have six children!" So that is how it works, I thought. So much for a woman's choice in the matter.

One afternoon, a discussion with some young men turned to the topic of Jim's and my marriage. Their question was whether Jim had paid a bride price of cows for me. Jim told them that marriage customs in the United States did not involve cows. I added, "If Jim had paid a bride price of cows for me, I would only want it to be about three or four cows."

The young men sitting in a circle were astonished. "Oh, Mary, you are worth a lot of cows. Why do you say only three or four cows?"

With a smile, I answered, "So I could do what I want!"

One of the young men jumped up from the plastic chair and paced around the outer edge of the circle, exclaiming, "And that is the trouble if you do not pay enough cows. She does what she wants." Then they realized that I was gently teasing them, and we all laughed.

Understanding the reasons behind some of the long-held customs in the Dinka culture contributed towards our not judging their culture harshly. For example, we learned that Dinka people believe that a man who has died continues to live through his offspring; therefore, a living brother will marry his brother's widow and have children with her in his brother's name. The book of Ruth in the Old Testament tells of such a custom. The incident occurred when Naomi tried to send Ruth, her recently widowed daughter-in-law, away. Naomi told Ruth that she was too old to bear another brother for Ruth to marry.

Ruth 1: 11-13—But Naomi said, "Return home, my daughters. Why would you come with me? Am I going to have any more sons, who could become your husbands? Return home, my daughters; I am too old to have another husband. Even if I thought there was still hope for me—even if I had a husband tonight and then gave birth to sons—would you wait until they grew up? Would you remain unmarried for them? No, my daughters. It is more bitter for me than for you because the LORD's hand has turned against me!"

Tracing the thread of the present-day Dinka custom of marrying your brother's widow to the Biblical story of Ruth and Naomi perhaps sheds some light on its origin.

A missionary who had done considerable research on the Dinka culture told us the bride price of cows had long ago been the way to ensure that wealth was redistributed and provided a way for a poor family to have resources when their daughter married. The ancient Israelites were also concerned with the redistribution of wealth by instituting a Jubilee Year every fiftieth year when debts were forgiven, land returned to the original owners, and slaves sent home to their families. These two ways of sharing the wealth within a society seem to me to have similar roots.

Jim's background in economics caused him to wonder if the Dinka's increasing birth rate would quickly outstrip any attempts towards economic stability. He and the young men who visited the school compound addressed this topic in some interesting conversations on Saturday afternoons. The Dinka men earnestly believed that each person who had perished in the twenty-three years of civil war needed to be replaced by a child, and to do so meant many babies needed to be born. Infant mortality was a stark reality as well. I observed daily how Dinka parents valued their children and how their children were a source of joy. Economic theories aside, we began to understand, given the history and circumstances in which the Dinka lived, why they believed the way they did about having many children. To be a barren woman in Southern Sudan would bring about the same shame and emotional distress as Hannah experienced in the Old Testament story found in 1 Samuel 1:1-28.

A practice that had a direct effect on me was the long-held custom that men did not prepare or carry food. To do so was an outright disgrace to the man. To prepare and carry food was the role assigned to women. "Isn't that convenient for men?" I commented to Jim, thinking it was one more thing men had created to keep women subservient. We had a friend named Gope, a bachelor of about thirty, who contrary to this custom came to the school on a Sunday afternoon, and in secret showed me how to make a flat bread called chapatti. We made a lot of chapattis, and I wrapped some up and handed the packet to him to take home. Gope was horrified at the idea, "If a woman saw me carry the food home, I would have a tough time finding a bride. Everyone would laugh at me."

I considered the custom strange, but then I thought about how the role of food affects relationships. As the only female staff member, without a doubt, I oversaw the food supply. If we had guests arrive near a mealtime, it was up to me to invite them to eat with us. The custom was never explicitly stated, but gradually I realized that I decided matters about food. As time passed, I experienced my control of the food as a place of trust and responsibility. In households, men planted and harvested, and then the food was given to the wives to prepare and share as they thought best. A wife's good stewardship in the use of the food directly influenced her family's well-being.

Linking Dinka customs to the Old Testament stories allowed Jim and me to be neutral in our judgments and to suspend deciding what was right and wrong in our neighbors' lives. I began to appreciate a pastoral culture that still had many things in common with those of past centuries. I realized that there might be reasons beyond my understanding that could explain things that initially appeared to me to be wrong or inappropriate. I imagined ancient people many, many generations before who may have been responsible for why some Dinka traditions are the way that they are.

#

Something happened to make Jim and me aware that our safety and well-being was a concern to our neighbors. One Saturday when the Toyota truck was broken, Jim and I started out on foot for the village of Akot six miles away to a place where we could check email. As we returned the six miles to school, a vehicle passed us going the other way. Seeing any vehicle was a rare sight.

It stopped, and a local official whom we had met months before emerged from the car and began scolding us for being on the road. Feeling like we were about eight years old, we stood in the middle of the dirt road astounded that this tall, broad Dinka man was angry with us. "Get in the car. Even though I am going the other way, my driver will turn around and take you to Atiaba." It was not a request but an order, and it seemed wise to comply. Once inside the car, the man brusquely explained there had been banditry on the road between Atiaba and Akot, and he did not think we were safe. We had to promise him we would not walk unaccompanied on the road. We had just experienced tough love, Southern Sudanese style.

#

Up and down the road that passed by the school, there were several compounds of missionary groups doing humanitarian work. Missionaries from the Dutch Reformed Church provided instruction in agriculture and business practices, Baptist missionaries planted churches, the Norwegian People's Aid distributed food, and the Mustard Seed Medical Clinic provided medical care with the support of churches in the United States. Catholic Loreto Sisters on staff at a girls' secondary school in Rumbek shared educational information with us. Jim and I became the newest additions with our work to open Hope and Resurrection Secondary School.

The missionaries whom we met had years of experience in the mission field, and they gave us good advice. They also gave us cups of tea, hugs, and stories that helped to fill the space where homesickness occasionally dwelled. We did not discuss theology because all of us knew there would be areas of disagreement if we ventured into theological topics. It was not that our personal beliefs did not matter to us as individuals, but the challenges in Southern Sudan required that we focus on the higher purpose of our being there. We all shared a sense of being called to mission and a dependence on God's guidance, and that was the strong bond between us. These missionaries from many various parts of the world were the source of many kindnesses.

Our chief partners were Jennifer and Darryl Ernst, founders of Hope and Resurrection Secondary School and their nonprofit organization, Hope for Humanity. When the money was being raised to construct the school, Jennifer and Darryl envisioned the school being handed over to either the Episcopal Church of Southern Sudan or the Ministry of Education of the newly formed government. It was soon evident that neither could administer nor support the school. They next turned to the US Episcopal Church to see if there were any missionaries interested in going to Southern Sudan to open the school, and this is where Jim and I came in. They entrusted us with their dream, and we trusted them to stand by us during that first year of operation. Jennifer and Darryl and the Board of Hope for Humanity were our rooting section and always ready to hear our news, good or bad, and be a part of the solution.

Also, our long-distance mentors were the staff of Mission Personnel of American Episcopal Church. They played a significant role in Jim's and my discernment to become volunteer Episcopal missionaries, and they provided our two-week missionary training. From the other side of the world, the staff of Mission Personnel stood ready to guide us as needed.

We had been led to believe that the United Nations World Food Program would grant our application for the donation of food so we could provide school lunches for the students. Our application, however, was denied even though Jim and I re-did the paperwork two times, visited the World Food Program offices in Rumbek, and hosted a visit to the school for officials of the World Food Program. The final word was that the people in charge of the World Food Program had decided to limit the food donation program to only primary schools. By the time we received word of this decision, school had been in session for over two months.

The more we learned about the living conditions of our students, the more urgent providing lunch became. The term applied to Southern Sudan is "food insecurity" which is another way of saying people are often hungry. Our students walked or biked about five miles one way to school, most often without having anything to eat at the beginning of their day or having any food to bring from home. Once at school, they were expected to learn a rigorous secondary curriculum on empty stomachs. Hope for Humanity's budget was already stretched, and no one had anticipated this cost. With each passing day, this problem became more pressing.

We stayed in close touch with our church community in California. Members of the congregation had already been generous with donations to Hope for Humanity for the operation of the school. I shared this information in a blog post:

> We think it will cost about $15 per student per month to feed them lunch, and we have about 50 students who regularly attend--$55 for each student will get us food through the end of the school year in mid-December. When Jim and I left home, many people said to us "Tell us if you need something." We do need something: contributions to help fund lunch. If this is something you can do

and that touches your heart, the address for Hope for Humanity is on this blog.

The following weekend, I sat in in the dusty, cluttered office of a neighboring missionary who let us check email on their Internet connection. I opened an email and read a message from a friend from church. "Woohoo! The vestry met and voted to send Hope for Humanity $4,000 for the lunch program. We did the math and decided that was the amount that you needed." Overcome with gratitude and so surprised that I couldn't speak, I pointed to the computer to share the news with Jim as tears streamed down my face. It did not matter that our church community was thousands of miles away. Their care for us and our work made it seem for a moment like they were just down the road.

The most important partnership of all was the one between Jim and me. Before we left for Southern Sudan, people counseled us about the kinds of stresses that would test our relationship. They warned that some marriages fail under the pressures of a mission. Jim and I believed we had already come through a test in arriving at the mutual decision to be volunteer missionaries in Southern Sudan. Our history together encouraged our confidence that we could weather the stresses.

I remember only one blow-up between us, and it was my blow-up rather than Jim's. In August, there was a month-long break for staff and students. Jim and I used that time to fly to Nairobi, Kenya, to rest and buy some things that we needed at the school. In packing to return to Southern Sudan, I must have left behind my pair of eyebrow tweezers. I tried to replace them at the marketplace in Rumbek, but people did not understand what I was asking until someone said "pinchers." I thought I was on to something by knowing the Sudanese word for tweezers was pinchers. It did not matter because there were no pinchers to be had.

Jim and I sat side by side on the bed in our room, and I poured out my frustration about being careless with my tweezers and not being able to replace them. The loss felt great. I had very few things for grooming, just makeup with sunscreen, a comb, and some hair ties. There were no comforts, just cold showers and a pair of glasses instead of my beloved contact lenses which I had left behind in California. I paced around the room and then left in a huff with the screen door slamming behind me. I stood outside in the sun, soon feeling very foolish. I took a deep breath and turned back to our room. I opened the screen door, "Jim, I am sorry for the way I acted."

Jim reached out his hand to me and compassion, understanding, and an acceptance of my apology were in his gesture. It was odd that a lost pair of tweezers was a flash point compared to the many much more challenging situations in which Jim and I had found ourselves. The mission experience was akin to putting our marriage in a kiln, and we emerged at the end of our time in Southern Sudan like a fired pot, shaped into a vessel that could hold our love for one another and some of God's miraculous grace.

#

One of Jim's dearest stories illustrates God's care of him and the safety that came from being a part of the community of Atiaba. The incident happened when Jim made a trip to Rumbek to the bank. We needed to pay the Kenyan workers and have money for building supplies for the construction of the teachers' quarters. Jim knew he needed to withdraw the equivalent of $5,000 US dollars.

Rumbek is about thirty miles from Atiaba, but the drive takes two hours because of the poor conditions of the dirt road. As usual, word spread that Jim was going to Rumbek, and about five people from the village asked to ride along. Jim assumed several people would want to ride back to Atiaba from Rumbek, but it turned out that no one who had ridden with him was returning to the village. These circumstances meant Jim was left to travel the two hours home by himself with an enormous sum of money in a plastic bag under the driver's seat. To be alone in the truck made Jim vulnerable to the known banditry in some areas between Rumbek and Atiaba.

When Jim tells this story, he says he prayed, "Lord this is for you. Please help me get back safely." As he was leaving Rumbek, Jim was flagged down by a man who told him that Chief Jacob and a few Atiaba officials were in town and would appreciate a ride back to Atiaba. I picture Jim's response as a huge smile and a vigorous nod of his head. The paramount chief's presence in the front seat and the others in the back ensured safe passage, and Jim's prayer was answered. Jim has always wondered if Chief Jacob had been praying for a ride home at the same time he was praying for company for the journey back to Atiaba. It is our experience God can be efficient to all involved when answering prayers.

#

In September when the Hope and Resurrection Secondary re-opened after a mid-year break, Jim and I got very sick. In the middle of the first night of being ill, I had to go to the latrine. I felt weak and dizzy and thought about waking Jim to go with me, but he was not feeling well either, and I decided not to bother him. A narrow sidewalk ran against the outer walls of the building of the newly built teachers' quarters. To steady myself, I walked slowly, half leaning on the wall. I was around the side of the building and across the back and had just turned onto an open expanse of sidewalk that covered the last ten feet when I fainted.

The next thing I knew, I opened my eyes and stared up at a black velvet sky glowing with glittering stars. I took in the beautiful sight and was relieved that I felt cool after being so feverishly hot. How did I get here was my next thought? I was lying on my back in a rain puddle on the sidewalk just a few inches from the latrine door. I gingerly got up and made

79

my way to the door of the latrine, and as I did, discovered that my left foot had been jammed against the outside wall when I fainted.

In the morning, I made my way into the kitchen and told Anthony and Cleous that Jim and I could not go to our classes that day. I returned to our room, and Jim and I slept, losing track of time. A knock woke us up. "Jim and Mary, a nurse from the clinic is here. Can you get up and come outside?" With difficulty, Jim and I got up and went outside to where Frances, the nurse from the Mustard Seed Medical Clinic six miles down the road, was waiting. It was morning break time, and the students were outside watching and murmuring concern and encouragement. I knew I looked a mess with my hair escaping from yesterday's ponytail and limping on my swollen foot. Cleous had to pick me up to put me in the truck because I could not climb in myself.

At the clinic, the nurse started IVs for Jim and me, and with complete trust in our caregivers, we gratefully swallowed the pills they gave us. As I drifted in and out of sleep, I thought I heard the Dinka headmaster's voice, but I dismissed the idea because I did not believe Anthony had made the round trip of twelve miles on foot in the heat of the day. Later I awoke to find my hospital bed surrounded by tall young men in Hope and Resurrection t-shirts looking at me. "You will get well. God will make you well," the students assured me.

The next day, Jim and I returned to school to rest in our room and continue to recuperate. When I went to the latrine, I carefully looked at the place where I had fainted. The sidewalk had been constructed on a slope, so there was almost a foot drop from the edge of the concrete to the ground. What had kept me on the sidewalk when I fainted because I could have easily fallen off to break my arm or twist my back or crack my head? How had only my foot been hurt when there was the potential for a more serious injury? I closed my eyes and remembered the sky from that night with the glowing path of the Milky Way reaching from horizon to horizon.

Once we had recovered, I was curious how Frances had known to come for us. Cleous told me that the news that Mary and James were sick passed up the road by word of mouth. It took from about eight in the morning until about eleven for word of our condition to get to the clinic and for Frances to come with the clinic's vehicle. I had not imagined hearing Anthony's voice when I was at the clinic because he had walked the twelve miles there and back. When I asked him about it, he replied, "I had to see if you and James would be all right."

#

As Jim and I developed relationships in Southern Sudan, we experienced what the bishop told the couple in El Salvador, "...those whom you will serve and love, and who will love you in return will keep you safe." There was an exchange of care and concern between us and our students and neighbors that had a way of equalizing relationships. We also experienced divine care, not easily explained but keenly felt, God's care of us.

Relating the chapter to your life: Recall an experience when something was accomplished because people partnered in the effort?

CHAPTER 4

QUESTIONS AND ACTIVITIES

If you are meeting with a group, take turns relating your personal story to one another that answers the following question. If you are reading on your own, record your story in your notebook.

Relating the chapter to your life: Recall an experience when something was accomplished because people partnered in the effort?

Chapter 4 shares stories about the many ways people depended on one another during the mission to Southern Sudan. We accomplished opening Hope and Resurrection Secondary through partnerships with God and people near and far. Jim and I based our Southern Sudanese friendships on mutual respect and trust, and interdependence on one another helped foster healthy relationships. Jim and I went to Southern Sudan to serve. Having a servant's heart was a good beginning, but that alone would not have allowed us to complete our work at Hope and Resurrection Secondary. If we had not embraced the community of Atiaba and joined our lives with the lives of our neighbors, our efforts would have most likely resulted in superficial accomplishments

Just like our life in the United States, Jim and I formed multiple circles of giving and accepting care and support while in Southern Sudan. The first was with the students of Hope and Resurrection. Jim and I gave our professional expertise and time and received from the students their effort and enthusiasm. Another circle of support was with our neighbors who welcomed us and watched over us, more than we realized at the time. We became part of the community by worshipping under Atiaba's tree church and facilitating people's care when they were ill by getting them to the medical clinic

The third circle of relationships consisted of the friendships of the missionaries serving in Southern Sudan. The exchange of stories and information with people whom we shared the bond of serving the Dinka people helped sustain our commitment to the mission of opening the school. Our family, friends, and church comprised our most distant circle of support, but their emails made us feel like they were not far away or separated from us.

Ecclesiastes 4:9-10—*Two are better than one, because they have a good return for their labor. If either of them falls down, one can help the other up.*

Hebrews 10:24-25—*And let us consider how we may spur one another on toward love and honorable deeds, not giving up meeting together, as some are in the habit of doing, but encouraging one another—and all the more as you see the Day approaching.*

The verses from Ecclesiastes tell of the advantages of being part of a community. The Hebrews verses describe how good relationships work. The advice is to be in fellowship with others for the good of all involved and offer love and encouragement to those around you.

The mindful recognition of the people who play significant roles in our lives often leads to the appreciation of their unique contributions to our physical, emotional and spiritual well-being. Praying for those who are a part of our lives, whether family, neighbors, friends, or colleagues, encourages thankfulness for them. It also challenges us to honestly acknowledge to ourselves any form of resentment we might have towards another. Prayerfully considering any negativity that we might be feeling towards someone does not necessarily change the other person but can change our understanding of the person so that we no longer need to make the negativity the focus of the relationship.

Record your responses in your journal. The reflection time is divided into two parts. Part 1 is creating a visual representation of the people to whom you give and receive support in the form of a mind map or web similar to the one that you created for Chapter 1.

Part 1 – Creating a visual of your "village" of support and interaction with others

In your notebook draw a center circle and four large circles around the center circle. See example.

- In one of the circles, record the names of people whom you mutually give and receive support and encouragement. These are the people with whom you share joy and sadness, and who might do such things as go to a doctor's appointment with you, keep your child overnight, or take you to the airport, and you would do the same for them.

- In another circle, record all the people who receive your support, but cannot give back to you in an equal way. These might be very young or elderly people or someone with a health concern.

- In another outer circle, record the names of others who are very generous to you with time and support in such a way that they seem to give more to you than you can give to them.
- In the last circle, record causes that you support which benefit people such as the charities to which you donate, ministries that you participate in at your church, and time and resources given to community things like your library or your child's classroom.

The activity is a way to access a lot of information, so move from circle to circle and back as the names of people are recalled. The format of your visual "village" of support and interaction will look something like this. Work quickly in any order that the names come to you.

Part 2 – Praying for the people of your 'village."

When you complete your visual village, consider the following questions. Focus on one circle of people from your visual village at a time.

- What kind of prayers might you say on behalf of the people named?
- What do you appreciate about each person? Can you include a prayer of thanksgiving for having the person in your life?
- As you think and pray, are there any negative things that come to mind—un-forgiveness, resentment, sadness? Are you willing to turn over those feelings to God?
- What do you think will be the biggest challenge in praying for your village of people? Are there ways to overcome that challenge?

If you are working on your own, re-read what you have written. Sharing your thoughts from the activity and questions with a friend is a further way to explore your ideas and get feedback.

If you are working in a small group, meet back in your group and as each person is comfortable, share any thoughts and insights. End the meeting with prayer and affirmation for the insights the group brought forward.

During the next week, continue to think and pray about and add any further insights to your journal about belonging to a village and the support you give and receive from others.

CHAPTER 5

Perseverance—Trusting God in the Face of Challenges

Isaiah 40:31—*but those who hope in the LORD will renew their strength. They will soar on wings like eagles; they will run and not grow weary, they will walk and not be faint.*

Hebrews 12:1-2—*Therefore, since we are surrounded by such a great cloud of witnesses, let us throw off everything that hinders and the sin that so easily entangles. And let us run with perseverance the race marked out for us, looking to Jesus, the founder and perfecter of our faith, who for the joy that was set before him endured the cross, despising the shame, and is seated at the right hand of the throne of God.*

The natural rhythm of daylight and darkness shaped our days. Without electric lights and with an increase of mosquitoes at sunset, we lived by the adage that begins "early to bed and early to rise …" Bedtime was about nine o'clock and jokingly referred to as missionary midnight by our missionary friends. Even after a busy day, I was not always able to sleep at nine o'clock, so I used the hours before I fell asleep for thinking, planning, and praying in the still darkness.

In contrast, my mornings were spring loaded. Instead of an alarm clock, I had the sound of flocks of doves walking around on the metal roof above me. The cacophony they produced was more like elephants in work boots rather than like little birds. I dressed quickly, for I had learned it was best to meet the day head on and be ready for whatever might happen.

The environment often acted as an antagonist, creating drama. The heat demanded a slow pace, and it was tiring to teach a lesson in the oven-like temperatures of the classrooms in the afternoon. In the rainy season, storms offered relief from the heat but brought activities to a standstill. If classes were in session during a rainstorm, the deafening noise of the rain on the metal roof made it impossible to hear. When dark, threatening clouds appeared near the time school was over for the day, we stopped classes early so students could get home before the intense, pelting rain began.

Snakes lived in the forest and bush surrounding the school. When Jim and I were in Nairobi, Kenya, we had gone to a reptile exhibit, and I was impressed by the superlatives that described the snakes such as deadliest, fastest, and most feared.

We had lived at the school for a couple of months without any sightings of snakes, and I put that kind of danger out of my mind. One evening as it was getting dark, I headed to the latrine. Jim said to me, "You should take a flashlight with you."

"Oh, there is enough light for me to see. I will only be a few minutes," I replied. As I opened it the latrine's screen door, I glimpsed in the dim light what looked like a stick draped across the square hole in the floor. In a flash of recognition, I realized that the stick was a snake. I slammed the door shut and screamed. The Kenyan workers who were building the teachers' quarters came running and killed the snake. They feared snakes and took the danger they posed seriously.

I went to Anthony and asked him if he thought the snake I had encountered had been poisonous. Anthony's answer was short, "It was from the forest." He did not invite further questions as if the snake being from the forest was all the information I needed to judge it poisonous.

I learned to pause before entering the latrine, and this lesson served me well when one day in late afternoon, again there was a snake in the latrine. This time the snake was a glistening green and yellow one, most likely a green mamba. Again, the Kenyan workers came to my rescue. When I told the students about this snake, they said, "James would not even have had time to drive you to get help at the medical clinic if the green snake had bitten you."

A small gray colored cobra was the third snake to pass through the school compound. Angelina, one of our female students, spotted it first and picked up a big stick and threw it at the snake. In response, the cobra turned towards us and brought about a third of its body off the ground and spread open its hood. Even standing out of range of its striking distance, I shivered in fear at the sight of the cobra.

I came to understand why babies and toddlers were never left unattended or put on the ground to crawl. I wondered how many people are bitten by snakes. From a statistical point of view, three snake encounters in ten months are not too threatening, but each encounter made me more alert to my surroundings.

#

Why were the decisions and challenges in Southern Sudan so difficult? Often it was because we lacked historical knowledge and a clear understanding of the future consequences of our choices and actions. It felt frustrating and uncomfortable to be stopped in my tracks without any Plan B available if the tenuous Plan A did not work. Never in my life had I been required to cope with things like a river flooding to keep me from going to town, or the Ministry of Education being months behind in providing a list of eligible eighth graders who were qualified to begin secondary school. Finding the bank closed during normal banking hours after making the two-hour drive to Rumbek frequently frustrated us.

It is not true that we had no options on which to rely because we always had prayer. Each day required effort and labor to operate Hope and Resurrection Secondary, and our dependence on God's guidance made our work meaningful rather than futile. We never thought of God as having a magic wand to solve all the problems instantly. Instead, we learned to count on the clarity and strength of purpose that we received from prayer.

Jim's and my focus had to be on our mission of opening Hope and Resurrection Secondary. The challenges such as food insecurity, lack of resources, disease, and threats of violence in the community could have easily defeated us. If we had focused on the things we could not impact, we would have drained our energy and effectiveness and eventually might have become resentful of those whom we had come to serve. We learned that perseverance was not only our determination to realize a goal but, also, included setting healthy boundaries. I closed a blog post with these thoughts:

Awareness and the beginning of understanding this community's needs can feel overwhelming sometimes, and it also means we must continuously discern the urgency and necessity of the many requests for help by the local people. Maintaining healthy, functional relationships is what we are striving to do. We are seen as rich because we are from America and have so many things here at the school including one of the few vehicles in the village. There is a tension to living in a culture so very different from yours—alertness that is necessary to understand and to react to others appropriately. That process is both exciting and tiring. We look in the faces of our earnest students, and we listen to them express the hopes they have for getting through Hope and Resurrection Secondary School. We begin to realize the magnitude of what they dream. We hope and pray that we can provide some of the foundation they need. Being in Africa is a humbling experience, and in truth, we offer so little in the way of help compared to so much need.

Seasoned missionaries advised us not to begin things we could not sustain like giving money and goods to people. Since many of the villagers had helped unload the truck of supplies from Uganda, everyone knew we had a lot of material things like big sacks of rice and beans, jugs of cooking oil, and luxuries like bars of soap. In an environment where people lacked basic resources and where the possibility of violence was always present, our neighbors had never had the opportunity to practice planning. Saving resources for the future was an impossible concept in the context of severe scarcity. As a result, it was inevitable that people came to us and asked for things.

With kindness, Jim and I told each person who asked for something that we were not free to share what we had because it was for the school and the students. Opening Hope and Resurrection Secondary School was what we were giving—giving of ourselves to be there and providing secondary education because of the generosity and efforts of hundreds of donors in the US. In the face of so much need, being asked and not being able to meet the requests was hard. The dilemma was holding the tension between being good stewards of the resources that had been committed to the school while being loving and helpful to the community in which we lived.

Our willingness to transport students and neighbors to the Mustard Seed Medical Clinic six miles away evolved as our gift. By sharing our vehicle and fuel, we acted compassionately to people in critical need. Jim monitored our fuel closely because we needed it to run a generator, and we always had to have enough to go to Rumbek to the bank and to purchase supplies including more fuel. Those things were not available in the tiny village of Atiaba. Jim managed in such a way that we could always drive people to medical care. He transported an old woman with a severely infected foot, sick babies and their mothers, children with malaria, pregnant women and our students when they were ill or injured. In this way, we became partners in the well-being of the community.

Very early one Sunday morning, some people came to ask Jim to drive a ten-year-old boy to the medical clinic. His name was Shedit which means Sunday. He had been bitten two weeks earlier by a dog. At the time, no one had known that the dog was rabid. When Jim returned from taking him to the clinic, he told me how very ill Shedit was, but how he rallied a bit at the thought of his very first ride in a vehicle. Although I did not know Shedit personally, I could easily picture him with long legs, a skinny body, and a huge smile because that is how the boys of the village looked. Late in the afternoon, some of our students came to tell us Shedit had died.

Anthony, Cleous, and Jim and I sat with the students, and we were all quiet. No one tried to comfort the others, or analyze what happened, or explain away the sadness. We shared the sadness—all of us in silence and solidarity. Sharing in the grief of the community reminded me that being compassionately present to others does not mean solving their problems or making things better. Instead, it is the willingness to share another's pain; even for a short while to be with another.

#

Working with the school's administrator, Anthony, taught me that creating positive working relationships with colleagues of another culture can be a challenge. Anthony is pencil thin and tall, and he had received his education before the civil war. He is thoughtful in making decisions and a man of few words when discussing an issue. In contrast, at five-foot-four inches, I am shorter than most Dinka people, educated in the US, quick to make decisions, and like to process ideas through discussion.

We were a partnership of opposites. The most glaring difference was gender because we were working in a society that has long had a fixed division of roles based on gender. I had a front row seat from the school compound to observe the women of the village, and to me, the division of labor appeared to be decidedly skewed in favor of men. It seemed men had a superior role in just about everything, and I let this become an annoyance. Because of my disapproval of what was required of women, I took Anthony's reluctance to discuss school matters with me as an affront. I was frustrated that this person whom I had to rely on to guide culturally appropriate decisions for the school was silent much of the time.

I wonder what Anthony thought of our first weeks of working together. He probably wondered what he got himself into by working with an extroverted, chatty, independent American woman who was always asking questions and sharing ideas. We were like dance partners out of sync.

During a school assembly, Anthony surprised me by giving me the title of Mother of the School. I knew Anthony was showing me respect by giving me this title because it is considered an honor to be a mother. Calling me Mother of the School was his way of making sense of my leadership and decision-making role at the school. I was an anomaly of sorts because

Anthony knew very few women in his culture who had the authority that I had. I appreciated his gesture, but his reluctance to discuss administrative issues continued to annoy me. Desmond Tutu says, "If you want to become an agent of change, you have to remember to keep your sense of humor," and I definitely lacked humor working with Anthony.

One morning, Anthony and I were alone in the school office, each of us working quietly. Through a window, I watched Elizabeth, the woman hired to cook and do laundry, hang Anthony's freshly washed shirt on the barbed wire fence. She had wrung the shirt out and had not smoothed out any wrinkles. In the breeze, the fabric moved precariously close to the sharp barbs of the fence. I got up and stood in front of Anthony's desk, "Anthony, Elizabeth hung your shirt to dry in a way that it will be wrinkled and torn. There is a better way to do it."

"It's OK," Anthony said, dismissing me without even looking up.

I felt a wave of anger because "it's OK" was Anthony's way of ending any possibility of a discussion, and his saying it to me caused me to recall all my past frustrations in one fiery lump of resentment. Standing before his desk and looking at the top of his head bent over his work, I felt like an exhausted swimmer treading water in a sea of negative emotions. But as I experienced those murky feelings, I asked myself an important question. Had I come to Southern Sudan to spend my time being resentful, or if I had come to do whatever was before me? This answer provided me with a different approach—one that let me lighten up on taking myself so seriously and contained some humor.

Taking a deep breath, I said, "Anthony, I tell you about the shirt as Mother of the School."

Anthony lifted his head and looked at me with a smile beginning on his serious face. He threw back his head and laughed and laughed. "OK, then show me about the shirt," he said. And I did, and the shirt dried with hardly any wrinkles and no tears in the fabric.

"Hardly any wrinkles" describes the respectful collegiality between Anthony and me that was launched that day with my lighthearted remark. The relationship was only possible when I laid down my defenses and judgment. Anthony and I went on to discover that by working together— and yes, talking things through—that we agreed about how to run the school. If you recall the story of his walking twelve miles round trip to see if Jim and I would be all right when we were sick at the clinic, you can measure the loyalty and friendship that grew between us. Working with Anthony required me to reach deep into myself and rearrange my perceptions and make space for another who was not like me.

#

Not all relationships are resolved, even with the best intentions. Samson, the teacher who had been hired to instruct math and chemistry, began having difficulty about halfway through the school year. Teachers qualified in math had been scarce when we were looking for one in Uganda, so we were relieved when our Ugandan friend located and hired Samson for us. Samson's education qualified him to teach math and chemistry, but he could not adapt to the Dinka culture. His manner seemed impatient and disrespectful to the students which resulted in escalating tension. Anthony had suggested changes, but Samson had not acted upon them.

Halfway through the school year, the students asked for a meeting with the staff. We met after school in a hot classroom crowded with agitated students from both freshman classes. The students' dissatisfaction showed itself in the buzz of noisy conversation. A student leader opened the meeting, and Anthony, Cleous, and Jim and I sat with Samson in chairs in front listening to students speak against Samson.

I focused carefully on what was being said because I knew that what was happening could have serious repercussions. We had experienced students getting angry and aggressive about how one of us teachers had marked a paper. We had tactfully dealt with the individual grievances, but this complaint from the entire student body was a different matter. Jim and I believed that most of the students had some degree of post-traumatic stress because they had grown up in the dangerous conditions of civil war.

I regretted that I had not been more aware of this trouble. I wondered how we, as a staff, could walk the thin line between addressing the students' complaints, and to use an expressive idiom—not throw Samson under the bus. I remembered that Jim had analyzed the math scores from the eighth-grade exit exam and determined most of our students had entered their freshman year with a math deficiency. I wondered if the students' frustration was because Samson was not providing the kind of instruction that supported their learning.

When it was my turn to speak, the students sat forward and listened attentively. I told them that either Jim or I would attend math classes as tutors to provide math help as needed. I had thought of this solution at the last minute to deal with the heart of their anger, which I believed was fear of failing. I had not consulted Jim, but a quick glance at him told me that he agreed. It was like letting some air out of a balloon, as my practical suggestion eased some of the tension. I knew it was a temporary fix, a Band-Aid when the situation needed major surgery, but for now, it gave us time to determine a solution. Mid-term exams were the next week, followed by a four-week vacation break. Cleous and Samson would return to Uganda to visit their families which gave us some time to address the problem before classes resumed in September.

#

Our biggest challenge was that most students were academically below the ninth-grade level. I continually modified lessons to fill in the students' gaps in knowledge and skills while still moving forward through the curriculum. In a blog post, I shared one of the possible reasons why students were behind:

> I often observe that some adults write their ideas in the dirt when they are trying to explain something, and that children write their numbers and alphabet in the dirt during church under the tree. The reason is that classrooms are still often held outside where the teacher has only a blackboard, and the students don't have paper and pencils and textbooks. People have grown up practicing lessons by writing them in the sandy soil around them. The lack of abundant printed material and the resources to write explains why students struggle with reading and writing.
>
> Offering a secondary curriculum with enough instructional support that the students can be successful has challenged us. In my English classes, we have practiced writing paragraphs for a few months, and it is just now that everyone can write a topic sentence, a paragraph body, and a concluding sentence. The lesson for us is to go slow, and it makes the moment when everyone masters something especially sweet. I have promised the students that we will progress to writing essays when we return from holiday, and they are eager to try this. I am grateful to have their desire to want to do well.

The planning done in the US before coming to Southern Sudan had not accounted for the hardships of the students' lives. Tardiness and absenteeism were the results of students having to come to school five or six miles one way by bike or on foot. Anthony delegated the granting of excused absences to me, and I struggled to be fair when students came to me. I turned to my belief that students gain maturity and good character when they share in the responsibility for their decisions and the consequences of their actions. I recorded an incident in my journal:

> This morning a student named Joseph came for permission to leave. I granted it but explained that missed work might be hard to make up—that only he could decide if his business away was important enough to miss school. I would support his decision, but he would be responsible for any consequence that would result from his absence.
>
> Obviously distressed, Joseph confessed that some of his cows had been stolen, and he was headed to the cattle camp to get them back. This action is not without risk for cattle camp behavior is like a black and white John Wayne movie. The tradition and the economy of cows are more real and tangible than getting a secondary education to our students which is why establishing this school is such an uphill battle.

I watched Joseph leave through the school gates, concerned that this intelligent, handsome young man would encounter the violence that was often a part of recovering stolen cows. The missing cows that he was seeking would someday be part of the bride price to take a wife, and that was not a little thing. I was relieved when he returned a few days later unharmed. Writing about the challenges helped me process what I was experiencing in a blog post:

> Of course, we started with the usual rules for the school, but then the reality of life in Southern Sudan caused us to be much more flexible in administering them. Very early on a Monday morning, a student knocked on our door to tell me that he had to miss school

that day because he had bought a bull in Rumbek on Sunday and needed to get it home to food and water. Sure enough, there was a young bull tethered in the school compound. That request was a light-hearted one, and it made us all laugh. Most often though, there are requests for permission to miss school for grave reasons.

A student named Abraham came to me, "Madam Mary, my brother's wife just passed a baby girl, and there is no food. Please permit me to go to other relatives to see if they will give us food. She especially wants tea." I slipped some tea bags and a packet of beans into his hand before he rode off on his bike.

Many students get malaria and are off to the clinic in another village for medicine and then home for a few days getting well. A shy, physically disabled boy had his head down on his desk. When I inquired if he was OK, he told me that he had to go to the hospital. I thought it was for him, but it turned out that he was not sick but sad and wanted to visit his sister in the hospital who had lost a baby the night before. You can see that this is not the usual situation that I am used to for running a school. The students and their hardships are teaching us in profound ways how it is to be a Dinka person living in this place.

I struggled most with how people used revenge against those who wronged them. I observed how our students were afraid to travel on the road to and from school during periods of unrest. Because the only people in our area were people of the Dinka tribe, we did not experience the tribal conflict that we would have if there had been other tribes in the area. The conflicts that arose were between clans, and they reminded me of the legendary feud between the Hatfields and McCoys. In a blog post, I tried to make sense of it for family and friends in the US:

There is unrest in this place, and at times the tension can be sorely felt in the students. Violence erupts in cattle camps between clans, and often results in injury and death and spills over into neighboring villages. Still practiced today is the ancient way of thinking that involves an eye for an eye. The spirit of revenge leads to much heartbreak in an already challenging place.

Many people were following our blog posts and praying for Jim and me. How could I share about the insecurity and still convey the hope that was also present? I didn't want those at home to only know about the violence, but also to know that many Southern Sudanese longed for peace. I searched for a way to articulate both my concerns and hopes in our blog posts:

As a kawaja (white person) I feel like I am in a bubble. I am a relatively safe observer, but it is painful to watch, to sit on the sidelines and see the results. We speak against violence in class; we pray for peace in school. Our students are transitional people. Their childhood and young adulthood steep them in the attitude of revenge, while their education pulls them forward to think in a broader, more forgiving way. It is not easy to be a transitional person for it is a tug of war of loyalties. I pray that we can offer a strong enough incentive for them to put away the ancient way of seeing their neighbors.

#

One night it rained for hours, and the early morning temperature was unusually cool. I was up earlier than anyone else and went out in the fresh air. The glistening wetness from the rain made everything bright and clean. I stood at the end of the compound taking in the scene, feeling a sense of peace. I thought of the students who would have trouble getting to school because of last night's drenching rain. Many students lived far into the bush and forest, and getting to the road would mean coming through water choked grasses as tall as a man. The gooey, wet clay soil of the compound reminded me of how difficult the dirt road would be to navigate.

The problems of absenteeism and tardiness were always before me, and this morning the rain would make the count of students absent higher than usual. But that was just a passing thought because the students were the focus of my concern rather than the administrative challenges. It had taken months to understand how difficult it was for the students to get to school each day because of distance, weather, and family obligations. I stood in the golden light of early morning with the mahogany tree towering above me, and birds singing wake up calls, and I began to pray for our students. I prayed for their protection, their future, their dreams, and about the hardships they endured. I prayed with thanksgiving, for I had come to love them.

Through the trees, I caught sight of four bike riders wearing gray Hope and Resurrection t-shirts. They must have started at first light to arrive this early. Now close to school, they sped up and turned the corner into the dirt lane that led to the school. They rode through the puddles and up to me. Their greetings were full of energy and joy. I felt my spirit rise fresh and renewed. With clarity so strong that it brought tears to my eyes, I knew the students were the prize—the precious prize of great worth, the reward for not giving up in the face of challenges and frustrations.

#

Persevering through problems and not letting annoyances and frustrations be a distraction took earnest prayers and seeking God's guidance. About six in the evening was a down time for me, as it was too soon to heat up the leftover rice and beans for supper, and in the failing light, too late to grade student papers. That was when I often journaled about the latest dilemma. The physical act of writing and the mental work of accurately describing a situation caused me to ask and answer essential questions.

Pen poised above the page of my journal, I thoughtfully considered what part I played in a current dilemma, wondered who needed compassion and support, and asked myself how I could be part of the solution. The process was like untangling a jumbled pile of ropes. Usually, I ended the journal entry with prayers for God's guidance. I like to think that the prayers were spot on, because by the time I recorded the prayer, my emotions were sorted out, and I could open myself to God's answer. I felt calmer, having a better understanding of the problem and feeling the assurance that the answer would unfold.

During each day, there were many arrow prayers. Prayers flung heavenward with urgency and haste. I prayed silently in the crowded classroom on the day the students complained about Samson. I prayed when Jim went to Rumbek on business. I prayed daily prayers of gratitude for our protection from snakes and malaria, for food in a place of food insecurity, and for our restoration to health after being sick.

Jim and I knew we were being prayed for by friends and family at home. When I returned home from Southern Sudan, a friend told me that she would sometimes wake up from a sound sleep at about two in the morning thinking of Jim and me. When this happened, she would pray for us until she fell back to sleep again. With a twelve-hour time difference between California and Atiaba, her prayers for us came during the heart of our busy school day, and I have no doubt that we needed those prayers.

Based on our experiences in Southern Sudan, Jim and I believe perseverance is not just grinning and bearing something or refusing to give up. It is much more creative than sheer willpower. If perseverance isn't combined with discernment, we merely wear ourselves out and miss the blessings God has for us. In the context of following Jesus, perseverance transforms our labor into a calling inspired by God, and we accomplish this calling through prayer and partnership with the Holy Spirit.

Relating the chapter's theme to your life: Recall a time when you were discouraged but persevered through whatever the difficulty was. Looking back to that situation, did a sense of God's presence have a part in your determination to not give up?

CHAPTER 5

QUESTIONS AND ACTIVITIES

If you are meeting with a group, take turns relating your personal story to one another that answers the following question. If you are reading on your own, record your story in your notebook.

Relating the chapter's theme to your life: Recall a time when you were discouraged but persevered through whatever the difficulty was. Looking back to that situation, did a sense of God's presence have a part in your determination to not give up?

Have you noticed that walking on a balance beam or maintaining the one-legged tree pose in yoga requires a constant focus and effort? Our life in Atiaba needed that same focus and effort to balance our multiple roles. Some days we were better than other days at balancing our administrative tasks at school while also responding to our neighbors' needs. When we failed to be all that we desired to be, what seemed to be important at the end of a day was our willingness to try again. Would you say the same thing about your life—that it takes constant focus and effort to balance your multiple roles?

Isaiah 40:31—but those who hope in the LORD will renew their strength. They will soar on wings like eagles; they will run and not grow weary, they will walk and not be faint.

Hebrews 12:1-2—Therefore, since we are surrounded by such a great cloud of witnesses, let us throw off everything that hinders and the sin that so easily entangles. And let us run with perseverance the race marked out for us, looking to Jesus, the founder and perfecter of our faith, who for the joy that was set before him endured the cross, despising the shame, and is seated at the right hand of the throne of God.

Isaiah 40:31 says we will not grow weary if our hope is in the Lord. In the passage from Hebrews, notice the words that tell us to whom we look as we run the race of our lives. Verse 2 says we are *"looking to Jesus, the founder and perfecter of our faith ..."* We are not doing the race by ourselves, for we have the care and guidance of Jesus.

Begin with the question that provides insights into your life circumstances and spiritual seeking. Proceed with the other questions as time allows. During the next week, continue to write in your journal to further develop your ideas on perseverance as it relates to the challenges you are facing. In your notebook respond to the following questions and ideas.

Question 1

Is there something in your life that *"hinders...and easily entangles"* you?

- Consider what habits, attitudes, and patterns of thought distract you from being aware of God's presence in your life?

- What changes can you make that will untangle you from things that keep you from being all that God intends for you?

- Reflect on the possibility of how untangling things in your life could *"renew your strength"* as the Isaiah verse states. How do you imagine things would be different?

Question 2

Think about the images from Isaiah 40:31 "...*soar on wings like eagles; ...run and not grow weary... walk and not be faint.* Choose the image that is the most vivid for you and take a few minutes to free write about what you chose. Write whatever comes to mind without editing or being concerned with grammatical rules or spelling. When finished, reflect on what you wrote.

Question 3

Reflect on the Hebrews passage *"...let us run with perseverance the race marked out for us."*

- What parts of the race (your life) inspire you? What possibilities are before you that excite you? Your reflections from Chapter 1 about a call to service might be helpful in identifying the possibilities.

- How can you think and pray about the things you have identified as necessary in giving your life meaning and joy?

If you are working on your own, re-read what you have written. Sharing your thoughts from the activity and questions with a friend is a further way to explore your ideas and get feedback.

If you are working in a small group, meet back in your group and as each person is comfortable, share any thoughts and insights. End the meeting with prayer and affirmation for the insights the group brought forward.

During the week, continue to think about what kinds of things require perseverance in your life circumstances.

TRUSTING GOD'S PRESENCE IN ALL CIRCUMSTANCES

CHAPTER 6

Nonjudgment—An Unexpected Ending

Psalm 98:9—*let them sing before the* LORD, *for he comes to judge the earth. He will judge the world in righteousness and the peoples with equity.*

Matthew 7:2-4—*For with the judgment you pronounce you will be judged, and with the measure you use it will be measured to you. Why do you see the speck that is in your brother's eye, but do not notice the log that is in your own eye? Or how can you say to your brother, 'Let me take the speck out of your eye,' when there is the log in your own eye?*

Typically, African schools take a holiday break about halfway through the school year which for us was the month of August. Cleous and Samson returned to Uganda to visit their families, and Jim and I used the four weeks to go to Kenya. Our holiday included going on an African safari and using our leisure time to work on recommendations and a budget for Hope and Resurrection Secondary's second school year. Jim breaking his ankle while we were on holiday was not part of our plans.

Jim was getting a cold and took some cold medicine on the day we departed the Masai Mara in Kenya where we had been on safari. The medicine had the adverse effect of causing lightheadedness. I was surprised when my usually robust, healthy husband fainted while we were waiting to catch a plane back to Nairobi. He crumpled to the ground, and in the fall, he broke his ankle.

Although Jim was in pain, we managed to get to the Mayfield Guest House where we were staying in Nairobi, and Jim spent an uncomfortable night. "Just find me a pair of crutches, and I will be fine," Jim told me the next morning, not wanting to believe that he had seriously hurt himself. Instead of locating crutches, I found out where the nearest hospital was and secured a ride for us. Six hours later, Jim had surgery to pin his broken ankle. Jim chose this over having a cast because having a cast meant follow-up visits. Returning from Southern Sudan to Nairobi for medical appointments would have been complicated and expensive. "It's my clutch foot," he declared to the doctor. "I have to be able to drive." Seeking serious medical treatment in Africa is something you hope that you will not need to do, yet from the moment we walked into the emergency room of the hospital every detail from the skilled surgeon to Jim's care in the following days was excellent.

While Jim was convalescing, we spent four days at a family resort on the Indian Ocean called Turtle Bay. I described our stay in my journal:

Turtle Bay is like a five-pound box of chocolates. We are not our usual, active selves because of Jim's ankle. We eat lovely food and rest. I take it as God's gift and willingly unwrap it. I do wish the students of Hope and Resurrection were playing in the waves of the Indian Ocean—they would love it.

When the four-week break was over, Jim was not using crutches and walking on his own without pain. We were rested both mentally and physically and looked forward to returning to the school. This time we were ready for just about anything that would come our way. I wrote:

Returning to Southern Sudan was anticipated with energy and eagerness. We immediately faced many of the challenging realities of life here on re-entry. The rose-colored glasses came off, and we rolled up our sleeves because this time we were not caught off guard by the difficulties. Samson did not return. He is afraid, he says. Just when I want to judge him for it, I wonder if he may have a point. It is perhaps best. Reconciliation between him and the students would have been so fragile that it soon would have shattered.

By his not returning, Samson solved the problem of the students' dissatisfaction but created the dilemma of where to find a math teacher in the middle of a school year in the heart of rural Southern Sudan. Anthony, Cleous and I looked to Jim, the only one of us who had a math background. Jim met our gazes, gave a big sigh and agreed to teach math. Jim now had the most demanding teaching load of classes per week even though he wasn't trained as a teacher. He wouldn't have been able to take over the math classes four months earlier, but teaching physics had served as on-the-job training for him. I sat in on his first class to encourage him but saw that was not necessary. I knew with certainty that Jim and the students were going to be okay.

During the holiday break, many of our male students had spent time in Rumbek and visited with friends and relatives who attended Rumbek Secondary School. When school resumed, a student named Isaac reported to us, "Our notes are so much better than those of the Rumbek Secondary students, and we are learning more things. We speak much better English than they do, and it is because of you, Mary and James, and all the American English you speak to us."

We began the second semester refreshed and with a clear and realistic idea of what we wanted to accomplish for the rest of the first school year. I described my hopefulness in the following way:

It is my nature to focus on what can be improved at school. I lean my will and spirit against the problems of absenteeism and attrition. I take a moment and step back to see the bigger picture—students working to understand math concepts, understanding force and pressure in physics, learning about the earth's cycles in geography, and trying to write multiple paragraph essays, to name just a few. When I view Hope and Resurrection Secondary School as a whole—from the first vision for the school combined with the generosity of donors, the dedication of staff and the efforts of students, then I can see that this first year of operation is unfolding like a miracle.

We had no way of knowing that the confidence we felt and the plans that we had made would be changed in an instant on a Sunday afternoon.

\#

Have you noticed that you can recall in detail a day when something of significance happened? Sunday, October 11, 2008, is one of those days for me, although the day started like any other Sunday. Jim and I had learned months earlier that church services began when we showed up, so we aimed at arriving about 9:30. We would linger over cups of tea, dress in our church clothes, and walk the equivalent of about two blocks through the village to the big mahogany tree that served as the place of worship.

School-age children were beating drums when Jim and I arrived at a nearly empty area under the mahogany tree. As people wandered in, the drums were taken over by adults, and the skinny logs that served as church pews gradually filled. I always sat near the young children who clustered around me and giggled while patting my white arms. The lay leaders began Morning Prayer, and the reading of Bible passages, and the sound of the drums and singing rose heavenward through the sturdy branches of the tree. We lingered after the service to shake hands and greet people, then we headed back to the school for a quiet afternoon.

Back at the school, the beans I had started that morning were ready. Anthony returned from visiting his family in Rumbek earlier than expected and ate lunch with us. Cleous had left a note on the kitchen table telling us that he had gone to the nearby village of Barpakeny with Father Anthony, a Catholic priest.

The previous week, Anthony, Cleous, and Jim and I had planned the remaining eight weeks of school and the final exams. Jim was going to start linear equations the next day, and he had spent time preparing how to get as much taught as possible in the time left. I was eager to begin a novel I had brought from the US. It was Richard Nye's version of *Beowulf*.[4] I knew none of the students had never read a novel before, and I was sure they would enjoy this ancient tale of heroes and monsters. Cleous returned

---

[4] Ibid.

about three in the afternoon, and since there was not much to do, the four of us sat in the shade relaxing.

A small group of local leaders arrived at the gate and hurried across the compound to us. The news they bore was shocking. People from one clan had ambushed people of another clan in the village of Barpakeny. Four people had been shot and killed. Like a mother hen with her chicks, my first thought was that Cleous had missed this dangerous situation by only an hour, followed by a sickening fear that those killed might be some of our students. We learned that none of our students were directly involved, but the violence affected the families of our students, and people in all the surrounding villages would soon be choosing sides based on clan affiliation and loyalties.

We were advised to stay in the school compound, and the day of the bad news we only ventured out to drive the six miles to use the Internet to send Jennifer and Darryl Ernst news of what happened. Anthony immediately knew that we needed to temporarily close Hope and Resurrection Secondary School because our students would not be safe on the road. On Monday morning, Jim drove Anthony to the village of Akot to inform the police to stop any of our students on their way to school and to send them back to the safety of their homes.

The affected area was several miles up and down the main road, and authorities feared the violence that had begun on Sunday afternoon would escalate. Five primary schools were closed, and no children played at the well or waved at us when we passed. Atiaba's and Akot's market stalls were shut up tight, and clusters of men stood in earnest conversation. We had not experienced this degree of unrest because before October 11th the insecurity had lasted no more than a few days and involved just a few people. Staying in the compound felt like being under house arrest, and the school was a lonely, deserted place without the students. There were no bikes under the trees, no sound from the metal rim that hung from a tree branch and served as our bell to mark the beginning and end of class periods, and no thud of the volleyball being hit back and forth with laughter accompanying a good serve.

With the school closed, one of the things I missed most was the student-lead devotions. These devotions occurred at the beginning of each school day, and the students took turns leading them. The prayers that the students said were extemporaneous and seemed to flow effortlessly from them. They prayed for the practical concerns of their lives—rain for gardens, safety on the road, and healing from malaria. The students also prayed for Anthony, Cleous, and Jim and me, and being prayed for by them felt like a gift. Their devotions ended with singing, and one of their favorite hymns was "I Decided to Follow Jesus."[5] Their African voices would raise with the conviction that there was "no turning back, no turning back." Now instead of the hearing the students' prayers, I was left to say my urgent prayers quietly to myself.

With time on my hands and stuck inside the compound, I reviewed some of the memories of the last eight months that were especially dear to me. One of those memories was when a group of women had come into the school compound ringing bells and singing. I had asked Anthony what they were doing, and he told me that they were the relatives of a wedding couple. They were out and about trying to gather "small money" and things like soap to give to the couple who were about to be married.

"Anthony, I have those things!" I exclaimed and ran to my room for some Sudanese pounds and a wrapped bar of soap. I presented my gifts to the women, and there were embraces and laughter. One woman had a drum and others had bells, and they gathered around me in a circle as they sang. The women began jumping up and down which is one of the ways

---

[5] Author, unknown. "I Have Decided to Follow Jesus." *The Assembly Songbook*. Broadmoor Press. 1959

they dance, and I copied their movements and joined them. Dancing connected me to them, and I looked at their happy faces, feeling happy myself. After the women had left, Anthony said to me, "It was good you played with them."

Remembering that happy scene of wedding guests dancing and singing just a few weeks before the trouble in Barpakeny was in stark contrast to this present situation which forced me to sit in the student-less, silent school compound. The good memory made the recent, deliberate violence almost impossible to believe.

Over the next week, there was more bad news. A soldier lost his life trying to bring law and order to Barpakeny. We learned that some people were so afraid of retaliation that the women, children, and elderly left their villages to go to their clan's cattle camps in the bush. It did not make sense to us that the conditions in the cattle camps with mud and manure made seeking refuge there the best alternative for people. Some of our students who lived in Atiaba spent nights sleeping in the forest rather than staying in their families' tukuls. They reasoned that they would be safer in the forest than being trapped in a tukul with no way to escape should people of an opposing clan attack.

We had become accustomed to seeing police and soldiers with automatic weapons, but now many civilians also carried automatic weapons everywhere they went. Jim, who had never expressed concern for our safety, told me, "There are too many guns." We prepared our backpacks with our passports, money, jackets, and flashlights, and we told Cleous to be ready to go with us if a situation seemed threatening. The river, the Bar Nam, had flooded a low place in the road due to recent heavy rains, and the overflowing river barred passage to Rumbek. Our friends at the Mustard Seed Clinic, who lived the opposite direction from Rumbek, told us to flee to them by making our way through the bush if we felt unsafe. We were all tense, and my insides felt like Jello.

116

Eleven days after the fateful Sunday, we sent the word out that Hope and Resurrection Secondary was re-opening on October 22. At the end of that day I wrote in journal:

Students came slowly. Just two of them for the longest time, and then a few more and suddenly there were 18 of them out of the 45 who regularly attend. The morning crawled by, and we didn't go by the regular schedule, but each of us took turns doing a lesson. Cleous told us that the students wanted to meet with us at lunch. After trying to piece together shreds of information from the stories we were hearing, we were glad at the prospect of hearing their points of view.

Cleous, Anthony, and Jim and I joined the students in a classroom. Taking turns, the students expressed their fear of harm as they traveled the road to and from school. Some told of seeing cattle keepers increasingly arming themselves for a fight in the future. The students' stated their comments respectfully and without drama. They worried that they were not safe, but they also wanted their Form 1 or freshman year to count for something. One student voiced his concern about what the American donors would think, and if they would discontinue support of the school.

The four of us stepped outside the classroom. "It's your decision, Anthony. Tell us what to do." It took only a few minutes to agree that we would release the students and the school year would be officially over. We would determine grades based on the work to date. On November 3, we would celebrate with a special lunch, and at that time the students could pick up their report cards.

To complicate the bubbling stew of emotions everyone in the area was feeling, Jim and I needed to tell the community and students that we were not returning for the 2009 school year. We had made this decision while on holiday break in Kenya and had planned to share the news closer to the end of the school year. Because of the violence between clans, the end of the school year was suddenly upon us, and our timeline for sharing our plans needed to be forwarded by several weeks. Our news of not returning for a second school year was often misunderstood and linked to the recent violence, even though we had made this decision prior to the civil unrest. People reacted with a combination of sadness, resentment, and even embarrassment by some who saw our leaving as a failure of the community. September 3, 2008, I recorded the following thoughts on our decision:

> Jim and I spent much reflective time examining our decision not to return after this school year is over. From Kenya (where we went on holiday), we could look at Southern Sudan from a boarder perspective. We drafted ideas and budgets for Hope for Humanity. We both think it is the best decision—we both think we are open to God changing our minds. We have been part of Phase 1 that included the school's beginning, the construction of the teachers' quarters, and the establishment of academic standards. It is an African school which needed American know-how. Jim and I have tried our best to give that. Phase 2 is for this African school to be able to function on its own, to be given independence and African leadership. We can leave the school in the hands of Africans because we have qualified people to take over. These people have God's blessings and the vision and gift of leadership.

We based our decision on many things. The most important reason was that Cleous and Anthony were excellent educators, and we believed they could assume the leadership of the school in its second year. It was right that Africans administer Hope and Resurrection Secondary going forward, and Darryl and Jennifer Ernst and the Board of Hope for Humanity would continue to guide and financially support them from the United States.

A personal reason was my concern for Jim. He had the most responsibility of all of us, especially for the maintenance of the school and vehicle, as well as teaching math and physics. He was worn out in a way I had never seen before. Our bout with the undetermined illness had left him with a cough that would not go away, and he had lost so much weight that his belt gathered the surplus of his waistband like a full skirt. One day I said to him, "You look old and skinny. How do I look?" With a grin, he answered back, "Old and skinny, too."

On November 3, the school cooks prepared a sumptuous lunch by Southern Sudanese standards—rice, beans and boiled goat. We were warned that the ceremony and lunch should be done quickly, since being inside the school compound could be a trap if anyone wanting trouble showed up. Only about twenty students attended along with local leaders, and we all gave speeches. The day was an emotional one for me, and the events did not feel real or like I thought it would. I didn't want a hurried ceremony, hollow speeches, and quick handshakes. As it got dark, individual students returned to school to say goodbye. Two stand out in my memory—Joseph and Abraham. Joseph brought a letter to us.

To father and mother of the school, James and Mary: Best greetings to you all in the name of our Lord Jesus Christ. Amen.

I am write this letter to you because you are going to leave and miss me and I miss you. Now I am crying although you can't see water coming out in my eye. I am crying in my heart. Madam Mary you are our best mother. We will not get another mother like you and like James. I think God is our way for you and me. God will sweep your way so that you will go safely to your continent. Thank you. I think you will remember me and if God able, I will meet you in another year like this year. Joseph

Another visitor was Abraham. Jim and I were surprised that he returned to say goodbye because he lived six miles from school and to come after dark posed some risk for him. He had lost both parents in the civil war and had served in the army as a child soldier. The difficult circumstances of his life had not left him bitter, and he was a kind and gentle young man. Abraham had found an old bike frame and over time scrounged parts until only the front tire was needed to complete the bike. Jim bought the tire for him. We admired his spirit and determination, and he looked to us like an aunt and uncle.

After saying goodbye, he held out his hand to me, and we walked across the dark compound. Southern Sudanese hold hands in friendship, and I liked having his hand in mine for those moments. At the gate, he said, "This is so hard," and I murmured a tearful agreement and said a blessing for him. And then he slipped out the gate into the darkness and was gone. I wrote in my journal:

Early last week the thought of a premeditated ambush of revenge on Dinka clan members by another Dinka clan disgusted me. I wanted to be away from this society that allows its members to engage in such behavior with the attitude of un-forgiveness and vengeance on its neighbors.

Last night when I couldn't sleep, I unpacked the feeling of disgust. I discovered that it is made up of fear for the safety of the students, the teachers, and Jim and me. Inside the feeling of disgust, I found sadness for the lives lost and the pain to the community. I was frustrated that the students were being kept away by the threat of violence, and they weren't in my English classroom reading *Beowulf.* There was also the disappointment that our time in Southern Sudan would end abruptly and negatively.

In my imagination, I found myself at the foot of the cross. When I gazed upward, I found that the cross was empty because I serve a risen Lord and his sacrifice on the cross was sufficient for me and all of humanity. I imagined running my fingers over the rough wood and knew with surety that Jesus's sacrifice included the Dinka people.

I could be fearful, sad, frustrated and disappointed, but I had no right to be disgusted for that necessitated a judgment on this society that is only God's to make. I long to see my Dinka neighbors as God must regard them—are they beautiful children still growing to understand things like forgiveness? Is God, who is not bounded by time, working out His plan for them?

As I thought and prayed, the image that came to mind was a sight I had once witnessed on the road in front of the school. I had watched a man herding his goats. His dress consisted of a traditional garment of rough cloth, and it resembled an ankle length nightshirt. In his hand, he carried a staff and about ten goats wandered ahead of him. As I watched him take long strides after his animals, I thought perhaps this was how Jacob of the Old Testament might have looked. During my time in Southern Sudan, I had learned some things about my Sudanese neighbors, but there were great gaps in my understanding of this pastoral society which has its roots deep in humankind's beginnings.

Was it naïve for me to decide that it was not possible for me to truly comprehend the complexity of the cultural differences and to give my confusion and heartbreak to God? In hindsight, I believe that it was my choosing the lens of God's love that made it possible for me to resist letting the violent situation color my regard for my Dinka neighbors and negatively influence my memories of the months at Hope and Resurrection Secondary. It required me to stretch my heart and soul, and in doing so, I made a space for the ambiguity and tension I experienced from not approving of parts of the Southern Sudanese culture while caring genuinely for our students and neighbors. My last Southern Sudan entry in my journal said:

> I have taken a few examinations that were so challenging that when I finished, I was not sure how well I had done. Africa and this mission to open Hope and Resurrection Secondary has been like one of those exams. I am not sure how well I have done. But like Mother Teresa said, "We can do no great things but only small things with great love."
>
> I think about Southern Sudan one relationship at a time— positive connections with real people who fed my spirit, and for whom I seemed to have made a positive difference, God has given me peace and knowledge that He sent us to the Josephs and Abrahams of Atiaba, and by His grace, we did a few things with great love.

We left Southern Sudan with almost empty suitcases because we gave away things like clothes, vitamins, books, and even my laptop which I left with Cleous to use for the next school year. What we took away were the insights and lessons that we had learned on the other side of the world. What did God and the Dinka people teach me in those nine months?

My Dinka students and neighbors taught me that it is possible to live with dignity even in harsh conditions. Children are nurtured, the elderly cared for, meals are prepared, laughter is shared, and conversations are lively and interesting. My Dinka friends are poor in material goods and opportunities, but they are always groomed and clean, their compounds swept, and greetings of welcome on their lips. The lack of resources does not diminish their dignity. Difficulties instill practical, mindful ways of meeting the hardships that have a unique grace.

I learned to be grateful. My neighbors lived precariously close to the edge of hunger and need. They were in extreme peril and distress when things happened such as their gardens didn't produce enough food, a family member contracted malaria, or a mother lost her life in childbirth. When something good happened, the good fortune was fully appreciated and proclaimed. The harvest from their gardens, the birth of a baby, recovery from malaria, the coming of the rainy season so planting could begin—nothing was taken for granted and God received the thanks. When things went wrong, God was not blamed. Their theology embraces God's goodness. Dinka people preface their remarks about the future with "God willing," because they acknowledge God's place in their lives.

When the students told me about attending a Sunday worship service, they did not describe it as "going to church" as I often say. "Going to pray" is the way they express their attendance at church. When we say we are going to church, it describes a designated place, whereas going to pray expresses the intent and act of worship. Their choice of words reveals how they communicate with God. Prayers are conversational and are about thanking God and asking for what is needed. "Going to pray" on a Sunday morning meant that a spiritual community gathered together, but it was not on a strict schedule that meant that the service needed to be over at a specified time. A Sunday church service was comprised of a sermon that taught a Bible story, the joyous singing of hymns that everyone knew by heart, and many announcements to share the community's news. I cherish this unhurried model of worship.

I discovered how the culture of the United States had encouraged me to be an impatient person. Rarely are my wishes thwarted in the US, and there are always many options when I want to go somewhere or have something. In contrast to my lifestyle in the US, there were many detours and frustrations in opening Hope and Resurrection Secondary. In the first weeks, my impatience took a lot of my energy and solved nothing. Over time, I came to understand that many of things I wanted and needed for the school were unavailable in Southern Sudan and that there was no way to hurry things forward for my convenience. I learned to re-direct my impatience to the things I could have and do within the circumstances of life in Atiaba. In this way, I mirrored the behavior of my students and neighbors in not becoming a victim of my negativity and frustration. One of the secrets to being fully present to a situation and people is not fretting about what can't be. When I practiced not worrying, I found myself able to focus on the possibilities directly in front of me.

When asked to summarize what my missionary experience taught me, I say: trust God, pray for guidance and clarity, use all the resources within yourself, and open your mind and heart to appreciate each detail of God's presence. My insight that God is in the surprises—that is absolutely and gloriously true.

Relating the chapter's theme to your life: From your own experience, a person you know, or a news story, share an example of someone choosing to accept another who is unlike themselves without being overly critical or making judgments without sufficient information. As a result, what was the outcome?

CHAPTER 6

QUESTIONS AND ACTIVITIES

If you are meeting with a group, take turns relating your personal story to one another that answers the following question. If you are reading on your own, record your story in your notebook.

Relating the chapter's theme to your life: From your own experience, a person you know, or a news story, share an example of someone choosing to accept another who is unlike themselves without being overly critical or making judgments without sufficient information. As a result, what was the outcome?

Chapter 6 is about the challenges of practicing nonjudgment. We need to practice making crucial judgments that affect our safety and well-being which is very different from being critical of others without adequate information and understanding. Prayer helps us hold the tension and ambiguity that comes from choosing nonjudgment in situations where our own experiences and cultural norms do not provide us with the information that we need to make accurate, informed judgments.

Psalm 98:9—*let them sing before the* LORD, *for he comes to judge the earth. He will judge the world in righteousness and the peoples with equity.*

Matthew 7:2-4—*For with the judgment you pronounce you will be judged, and with the measure you use it will be measured to you. Why do you see the speck that is in your brother's eye, but do not notice the log that is in your own eye? Or how can you say to your brother, 'Let me take the speck out of your eye,' when there is the log in your own eye?*

The verse from Psalm 98 assures us that God's judgment will be fair. In contrast, the passage from Matthew warns us that if our view of others is harsh and self-serving, we can expect the same treatment from God. The parable of the Pharisee and the tax collector found in Luke 18: 9-14 adds another reason to avoid the unfounded judgment of others.

Luke 18:9-24—*To some who were confident of their own righteousness and looked down on everyone else, Jesus told this parable: "Two men went up to the temple to pray, one a Pharisee and the other a tax collector. The Pharisee stood by himself and prayed: 'God, I thank you that I am not like other people—robbers, evildoers, adulterers—or even like this tax collector. I fast twice a week and give a tenth of all I get.'*

"But the tax collector stood at a distance. He would not even look up to heaven, but beat his breast and said, 'God, have mercy on me, a sinner.'

"I tell you that this man, rather than the other, went home justified before God. For all those who exalt they will be humbled, and those who humble themselves will be exalted."

Jesus is teaching that the overly critical judgment of others will result in being self-righteous, especially when we believe others compare unfavorably to us. A self-righteous person's attitude of superiority prohibits compassionate responses to others. Self-righteousness closes us to God's call and guidance and keeps us from an honest self-examination of our motivations and actions. For example, we might have unfavorable judgments about how someone parents children, takes care of health matters, or manages finances as compared to how we do those things. When we view another person in a narrow, critical way it makes us feel superior. Being critical of others keeps us from recognizing and appreciating people different from ourselves

Review the questions and begin with the question that will provide insights into your life circumstances and spiritual seeking. Proceed with the other questions as time allows. Reflect on the following questions and record your thoughts and answers in your notebook.

Question 1

Re-read the parable from Luke about the Pharisee and the tax collector.

- Reflect on a time that you acted like the Pharisee by feeling superior to another. Consider that this might have occurred in seemingly small things like engaging in gossip or being dismissive of a person or not inclusive.
- Reflect on a time that you were like the tax collector, and another person disregarded you in some way.
- What are your take-aways or personal lessons for the future from experiencing the roles of the Pharisee and the tax collector?

Question 2

Why do you see the speck that is in your brother's eye, but do not notice the log that is in your own eye? Or how can you say to your brother, 'Let me take the speck out of your eye,' when there is the log in your own eye?

- If you heeded the advice given in the passage from Matthew, what changes in thought and attitude would be required of you?

- How might some outcomes in your life be different if you did not engage in unfair or unfounded judgment? What positive thoughts could replace the negative ones, and how would you think and pray about it?

Question 3

Re-read the verses from Psalm: 98:9 - *let them sing before the LORD, for he comes to judge the earth. He will judge the world in righteousness and the peoples with equity.*

What words or phrases do you notice? Take a few minutes to free write about what this Psalm is saying to you. Write whatever comes to mind without editing or being concerned with grammatical rules or spelling. Re-read what you have written and notice any insights that are new to you.

If you are working on your own, re-read what you have written. Sharing your thoughts from the activity and questions with a friend is a further way to explore your ideas and get feedback.

If you are working in a small group, meet back in your group and as each person is comfortable, share any thoughts and insights. End the meeting with prayer and affirmation for the insights the group brought forward.

During the week, continue to think about judgments that are based on compassion and facts. Add any further insights to your journal.

CHAPTER 7

Hope and Faith—Once a Missionary, Always a Missionary

Micah 6:8—*He has shown you, O mortal, what is good. And what does the* LORD *require of you? To act justly and to love mercy and to walk humbly with your God.*

Matthew 5:14-16—*"You are the light of the world. A city set on a hill cannot be hidden; nor does anyone light a lamp and put it under a basket, but on the lampstand, and it gives light to all who are in the house. "Let your light shine before men in such a way that they may see your good works, and glorify your Father who is in heaven.*

We returned to Northern California on November 7, 2008. Our son, Mark, surprised us by driving from Fresno and was waiting on the porch when we arrived home from the San Francisco airport. What a joy it was to have Mark be among the first to welcome us home. On our first Sunday back, we attended church services at our home church, and the reception we received was beyond anything we expected. People put their arms around me and did not let go. As they held me, they whispered loving things, "I was praying for you. It is so good to have you home safely." Jim and I traveled to Southern California to see Matthew and Samantha, our son and daughter-in-law, and while we were there, we went to Sunday services at Matthew's church. We were welcomed warmly as Matt's parents and realized that we were not strangers because the congregation had been praying for us at Matt's request. Our homecoming from Southern Sudan provided an appreciation of how many people care for us.

The damage from the house fire many months earlier had been repaired. The insurance company had discarded all our small appliances as unsafe because of the heat from the fire, and we had a generous check to cover replacing them. The holiday season was in full swing, so when we shopped for the things we needed, it was amid all the Christmas shoppers. We were overwhelmed by the abundance of all the choices and the decorated stores which were in contrast to the lack of resources and the rickety market stalls that we had experienced in Southern Sudan. Although we needed quite a few things, we found the stores so distracting that we only managed to purchase one thing at a time. Jim and I would make a single purchase of a toaster or hair dryer and then stop at Starbucks to quietly drink our coffees and watch people come and go. Most public places seemed loud and distracting compared to the pastoral setting of Atiaba. When friends asked me about our time in Southern Sudan, I found that it was hard to articulate the complex combination of grief for the friends left behind in Southern Sudan and the relief to be safely home.

I reviewed my journal from Southern Sudan to help me process the mission and re-entry back to the US. I found the following journal entry about a team from the US who had visited the school in the second month of the mission:

Among the treasures left behind by the short-term mission team from the US was a magazine called *Back Yard Living*. Within its pages, I read how to have a perfect container garden which is in stark contrast to the pair of oxen pulling a plow to prepare the field next to the school for cultivating groundnuts (peanuts). No container gardens at all in Southern Sudan, let alone a perfect one.

How might I be different when I return to the US? I am not entirely sure, but I hope that I am capable of some changes while also enjoying the conveniences of American life. What I wish for is not to strive for a perfect container garden or any other contrived standard of the good life. Can my African experience inform how I spend my time and money? How can it not, is my prayer?

Jennifer and Darryl Ernest of Hope for Humanity kept us informed about the recent news from Southern Sudan. I thought a great deal about Hope and Resurrection Secondary School and the students and the residents of Atiaba. My head and heart were suspended in no man's land, halfway between Southern Sudan and the United States. On Dec 6, I wrote a final post for the Southern Sudan blog:

What is next for Hope and Resurrection Secondary in Southern Sudan? We are receiving news of progress made in reconciliation between the two clans. The men responsible for inciting the violence have been turned over to the police. This is key, for to practice justice through the law eliminates the need for revenge. Until this incident occurred, I had not appreciated the friendship and cooperation between our students of different clans. It shows that there are many Sudanese ready to embrace change that will move them forward. The school year in Southern Sudan is from

April to December. The funding NGO, Hope for Humanity, is planning on a 2009 school year. Anthony, our headmaster of last year, is returning and Cleous, the teacher from Uganda, will become assistant headmaster. This year's freshman will become sophomores and a new class of freshman will be admitted. The setback of this year's early closing does not discourage us. Hope for Humanity needs your continued partnership of support and donations for theirs is an important and huge undertaking.

Home - Jim and I arrived in San Francisco on November 7th. We have spent this last month visiting our sons and Jim's sister and catching up with friends. We have begun to put our house in order from the fire. We have spent a lot of time remembering the details of these last nine months, the frustrations, challenges, the funny things, and joys. People have made our homecoming a celebration and encouraged us to talk about our experiences.

We are grateful for the blessings of our life here, but we also left a hunk of our hearts in Atiaba, Southern Sudan. Books on mission emphasize the practice of being present to the people you serve and that is difficult to understand until you are in a faraway place sharing in the lives of others. The richness of the last nine months is present in our affection for the students and staff of Hope and Resurrection Secondary School and that we share with them the experiences of the birth of the school.

Thank you, Dear Readers, for your interest. We heartily recommend being missionaries and are more convinced than ever that our lives are designed to be lived in service to others near or far. There lie our satisfaction and delight.

We settled back into our life in California. Through writing and speaking, I told the story of the school's first year, and Jim and I participated in fundraising for Hope for Humanity. For the next five years between 2010 and 2014, we went to Kenya annually for about a month at a time to present teacher training workshops to primary teachers, and in that way continued to be a part of missionary work in Africa in education. It was rewarding to work with the Kenyan teachers, but it never engaged my heart to the extent that being Mother of the School at Hope and Resurrection Secondary had.

Jim and I believed that it was not wise to visit Atiaba and Hope and Resurrection Secondary School until Anthony and Cleous had an adequate amount of time to establish their authority and way of administering the school. In May 2013, Jim and I accompanied Jennifer Ernest and another Board member of Hope for Humanity to South Sudan.[6] I wrote the following in anticipation of returning to the school:

> This week I have felt about five years old and like I was waiting for Christmas to arrive. May 12, we leave for South Sudan, and I am excited. What sets this trip apart from the other trips to Africa is the sense of a homecoming that comes from returning to people and a place we know well. It has been five years since Jim and I spent the first school year of Hope and Resurrection Secondary School in the village of Atiaba, South Sudan.

I described our homecoming to the school in a blog post:

> On Monday, I attended an assembly at Hope and Resurrection Secondary School. As a guest, I sat in the front with the perfect

---

[6] In July 2011, the people of Southern Sudan voted for independence and became the Republic of South Sudan.

view of all the students before me, two hundred young people in blue shirts and gray skirts or trousers. There were speeches, songs, and laughter.

I looked beyond where we were sitting in a covered pavilion that is new since our first year, across the compound to the other new buildings. In the background, I watched the three lunch ladies gathering firewood and beginning preparations for feeding two hundred students rice and beans at 12:35—on the dot without the benefit of a clock. On the far corner of the grounds, workers are building the girls' dorm from burned bricks made at the school in a rustic kiln.

Outside the school fence, the bush surrounds us with tropical trees, and the dirt path to the school meets the rutted, dusty road. In the distance tukuls with thatched roofs, cooking fires, and jerry cans of water from the well are the things that make up the daily life of the citizens of rural South Sudan. Inside the school compound, students learn about the world beyond the forest and the dusty road, and I marvel at the progress since Jim's and my first year at the school. Six years ago, the students wore Hope and Resurrection T-shirts, I slept in a classroom, and we were a staff of four. The contrast of the students looking sharp in their uniforms, a staff of twelve teachers ready to begin a week of instruction, and the additions to the compound and the construction of the dorm feel like major triumphs.

When we first arrived at the school on Thursday, greetings and handshakes welcomed us. When I got to Anthony, he embraced me which is uncharacteristic for his conservative manner. I found myself crying the kind of tears that flow freely and will not stop quickly. I think the tears came from a deep well of memories from the first year at the school and were prompted by the joy on Anthony's face and responding with my own pleasure at seeing him. I am glad to be here—all is well.

The visit went quickly, and there was work for us to accomplish—interviews with students, photographs, and academic and personnel issues to discuss. Joseph, our former student and the writer of the beautiful letter to us when we departed in 2008, came to see us. Joseph had been Jim's height at six feet three when we left, and now he was a head taller than Jim. Joseph is teaching at a primary school down the road. We asked about our dear Abraham and learned that he had joined the army. The paramount chief's son, Gabrielle, who had been one of our brightest students, traveled all the way from Juba to see us. A favorite story is about a gifted math student named Thon. After he graduated, he taught math to seventh and eighth graders at a local primary school, and until he joined the staff, there had been no one qualified to teach math at the upper-grade levels. In South Sudan being a graduate of secondary school has the status that is close to the equivalent of having a bachelor's degree in the United States.

On Sunday morning, we walked to a local church. There we found Joseph and our former head perfect, Isaac, leading the singing. Many of the current Hope and Resurrection students were in attendance and helping with the worship service. I felt the surge of pride that our graduates and students were assuming places of responsibility in the community.

Dennis, the Ugandan teacher who teaches English, was recovering from malaria, and Anthony asked me if I would take a few of his classes. The day's lesson was on idioms, and I drew pictures on the blackboard to illustrate "a chip off the old block" and "a wet blanket." The favorite drawing was my version of "burying the hatchet." In Senior 2 English (sophomore class) I chose a piece from their literature book about the importance of myths. The students were curious about me, a person whom they had heard about which resulted in my having their complete attention during the lesson. Jennifer Ernst related a comment Anthony made to her when she had told him that I looked happy to be back in the classroom. Anthony told her that I seemed pleased because I was a good teacher. Anthony's affirmation of my competence and the opportunity to be in the classroom were highlights of the trip. I wrote of seeing the progress on the construction of the girls' dorm:

> Seeing the nearly finished girl's dorm is seeing a dream realized. The Ugandan engineer overseeing the construction decided that the widely used mud bricks would not provide permanence. The teachers and local workers built a rustic kiln to fire the mud bricks, making them more permanent. The teachers also pitched in to dig the trenches for the foundation. The girls are very excited at the prospect of living in the school compound.

One afternoon, I sat in a plastic chair in the shade of the mahogany tree with Anthony. One of the stories he told me was how the competition for jobs is so great that employers give exams to determine the top candidates, and Hope and Resurrection graduates have been the top scorers and therefore earned the jobs. Anthony expressed it this way: "They say when people see our students are sitting for the job exams, they just run away. People used to think Atiaba was just a place in the trees, but now they know it is the place of Hope and Resurrection Secondary."

The Ugandan teachers are not missionaries in the formal way Jim and I were, but they are missionaries in their hearts and attitude toward the work of educating Dinka young men and women. Any administrator will tell you that a school is only as good as the quality of the teachers and their instruction, and Hope and Resurrection Secondary has a staff comprised of outstanding individuals in both their personal and professional lives.

In 2008, as we were leaving the school, Jim took two small mahogany boards that were left over from the construction of the teachers' quarters, and once home, Jim made small crosses from this wood. At a teachers' meeting the last day of our visit, he presented a cross to each member of the staff as a parting gift. Jim told them he was returning the mahogany boards to their rightful place in South Sudan.

Hope and Resurrection Secondary School is located in the part of the world where there is lack of resources and widespread illiteracy—a wilderness of poverty. The school has provided a reference point for success and progress for the communities it serves. The young people of the graduating classes to date are some of the best-educated citizens in South Sudan.

American Episcopal priest, Rev. Paul Johnson, experienced first-hand the unfolding of the dream of a secondary school in South Sudan. Rev. Johnson visited Southern Sudan on short-term mission trips while the school was being constructed in 2005 and 2006 and returned to visit a third time in 2012 to see the school in its fifth year of operation. In a video interview,[7] he eloquently describes the sense of divine purpose one feels when visiting there. Rev. Johnson calls Hope and Resurrection Secondary a beautiful miracle where young people have a chance to grow and mature and create a future for their nation. He says that the school is "a vital, life-changing, world-changing, kingdom-bringing-in kind of ministry."

Hope and Resurrection Secondary School is co-educational, and in recent years about forty percent of the student population have been girls. Having so many girls is remarkable in a country where only two percent of

---

[7] You tube at https://www.youtube.com/watch?v=vJBj8ggDsKM or Hope for Humanity, Inc. website at http://www.hopeforhumanityinc.org.

all secondary age girls attend school. The idea of gender equality promoted at the school has provided its students with attitudes of mutual respect between female and male students which is new to their culture. Preparing girls through education to play positive, active roles in their families, communities, and country is a stabilizing influence for the world's newest nation.

The civil unrest that began in December 2013 has filled the media with horrific stories of suffering, hunger, and violence. There are times when it is difficult to go out and tell Hope and Resurrection Secondary's story because the future looks precarious. When we are saddened and discouraged with the political situation, Jim and I remind ourselves that it is not for us to give up and that the teachers and students need our prayers and encouragement as never before.

Hundreds of local people walk or bike to the graduation ceremonies at Hope and Resurrection Secondary each December. The surrounding communities value the school, and people are uniting to keep it safe even in turbulent times. In 2016, USAID and VISTAS International hosted a three-day conference on peace at Hope and Resurrection Secondary, and secondary students from other schools came to participate. The students learned about peace the first day and presented what they learned to their parents and community members the second day. The last day culminated in a peace march to a nearby village. This current generation of secondary students is being prepared to play critical roles in bringing about reconciliation and peace in South Sudan.

The motto of Hope and Resurrection Secondary is from Matthew 19:26 *"With God all things are possible."* In the school's first year of operation, the motto proved to be true and has remained true even in the face of violence and civil unrest of the last few years. To date, nothing, even warring governmental factions, has stopped the education of students.

Occasionally, one of the hymns for the Sunday service at my church is "I Have Decided to Follow Jesus". I am instantly taken back to Hope and Resurrection Secondary and the student-led morning devotions. I do not hear the voices of the choir and congregation around me, but instead, I remember the African voices of the students. Jim reaches for my hand while the memories of the school are so sharp they overtake me. When the chorus comes with the words "no turning back, no turning back" my resolve is strengthened to support Hope and Resurrection Secondary in any way that I can. I am reminded that following Jesus cannot be done halfway because the dedication and passion needed to be an agent of positive change in our troubled world take a wholehearted effort.

From time to time, I take out a bundle of poems written by students of Hope and Resurrection Secondary on our 2013 trip. A girl named Rebecca writes in her poem of her desire that her life stands for something good.

I understand I am instrumental

I say let me serve all

I dream of how I make others feel good

I try to see all the good results

I hope I am of great value

I am healthy and strong.

Her words inspire me to continue to believe that something extraordinary is happening at the school. I say, "Yes, Rebecca, you are of great value."

\#

When the mission was over in Southern Sudan, and later our work was finished in Kenya, I asked myself if I was still a missionary. The resounding answer was, of course, I am still a missionary and will always be if I expand the way I think about service to others. Most often the word "missionary" elicits thoughts of someone going off to faraway places, but I invite you to think about being a missionary in more ways than that narrow definition. Often the mission field is not on the other side of the world but with our neighbors down the street, in the soup kitchen in our city, or with a troubled member of our family. Each of us is called to a daily mission of service wherever we find ourselves, and an incident that occurred after we were home from Southern Sudan affirmed that truth.

After a Sunday church service, I hurried down the wide hall of my church to the coffee hour where I hoped to catch up with a person whom I needed to talk to about a church activity. Going in my same direction, but much more slowly was Alice, an elderly woman who was making her way with her walker. As I passed her, I turned and greeted her with the plan to then go quickly on my way, but Alice surprised me by stopping in the middle of the hall. I had no choice but to pause also, for not to do so would have been rude. We stood side by side with the crowd streaming around us, and I thought to myself how I would now miss the person whom I had hoped to make contact.

Alice's pastel blue blouse matched her eyes, and she peered at me through her silver-rimmed trifocals. She said, "Today is the tenth anniversary of my husband's death." The combination of her statement and how vulnerable she looked leaning on her walker caused me to forget about the person I wanted to see, and I gave my full attention to her. Alice then told me a story about her husband, and it was a lovely story about the man with whom she had spent most of her life.

When I thanked her for telling me the story, Alice replied, "When I came to church today, I knew I wanted to tell someone that story about my husband. Mary, I am glad that it was you."

"Me, too," I said with a hug. As I walked away from Alice, I knew that I had felt exactly like this once before, had felt awe and honor that I was in the right place, at the right time. Then I remembered the red dirt schoolyard in Southern Sudan and my student, Mabor, saying to me, "We say that you are our teacher and we are so proud." Just as with Mabor, I felt humbled and grateful to be granted the unexpected privilege of sharing in a moment of Alice's life.

I chose to recount a sweet moment of connection with another person to illustrate that you don't have to go to Africa to discover that God needs your gifts and willingness to participate in His mission in the world. God's world is everywhere. The experience with Alice was a spur of the moment opportunity to make myself available to give compassion and encouragement to another person. It was easy to say "yes" to sharing kindness with Alice. Not all calls on our time and talents are as easy as it was to respond to Alice. Sometimes we are presented with situations that can use what we have to offer, but we find that saying "yes" presents challenges. To say "yes" to a mission, near or far, often means changes need to occur and things are given up. Not only do we have to forsake comfortable and familiar things, but at the same time, we must be willing to embrace new people and unfamiliar circumstances that will be brought into our lives because of our choosing to engage in God's mission in the world.

To be a missionary meant that I had to leave my American students to go to Southern Sudan, and that required I forego income and security and let go of something I liked doing. My discernment to retire early from teaching took careful consideration, and for a while, I vacillated between wanting to pursue my desire to be a missionary and staying where I had safety and comforts. When we perceive a tug at our hearts or envision a new path of service, we are required to trade what we know for the unknown.

The idea I appreciate the most is that God extends to each of us the choice to engage in His mission in the world, and that invitation is always open to us. New possibilities continue to be offered to us again and again when we are mindful of them. On our part, we have to trust that by following Jesus we will gain meaningful purpose and connections with others, and our hearts and minds will be transformed in ways that will make our lives complete and satisfying. Micah 6:8 expresses this idea eloquently and simply: *And what does the* LORD *require of you? To act justly and to love mercy and to walk humbly with your God.*

#

Consider the overarching question that was asked in the introduction of the book: Can the lessons taught by God and the Dinka people of Southern Sudan be brought home to the United States and applied here for a life that is more abundant and generous?

An overview of the lessons that I learned includes recognizing the dignity of others, gratitude for all things, patience and perseverance in challenging circumstances, and being present to others. Also, I learned that seeking clarity and strength through prayer was an absolute necessity. I experienced accepting the ways of another culture without imposing my US values and norms on my hosts. I like to think I left Southern Sudan as a more authentic person, aware of my inadequacies but not paralyzed by them, as well as knowing some of the skills and abilities that I have to offer God and others.

For you to decide the worth of the lessons from the other side of the world as applied to your life circumstances, it is helpful to define the words "abundant" and "generous" in secular terms and the context of God's Word.

"Marked by great plenty; ample" is the definition of abundance. The following Bible passages help us understand an abundant life in Christ includes joy, peace, hope, God's presence with us as His children, and empowerment to accomplish God's mission in the world.

- John 10:10 states: *The thief comes only to steal and kill and destroy; I have come that they may have life, and have it to the full.*

- Romans 15:13 says that abundance will come in the form of joy, peace, and hope. *May the God of hope fill you with all joy and peace as you trust in him, so that you may overflow with hope by the power of the Holy Spirit.*

- In the passage, Revelation 3:20, we read that abundance includes having the attention and presence of Jesus in our lives. *Behold, I stand at the door and knock. If anyone hears my voice and opens the door, I will come in to him and eat with him, and he with me.*

- John 1:12 promises the birthright of becoming children of God. *But to all who did receive him, who believed in his name, he gave the right to become children of God.*

- Ephesians 3:20-21 assures us that through God there is a power in us that can accomplish things beyond our imagining. *Now to him who is able to do far more abundantly than all that we ask or think, according to the power at work within us, to him be glory in the church and in Christ Jesus throughout all generations, forever and ever. Amen.*

"Magnanimous; kindly; characterized by a noble spirit" is the definition of generous. Scripture describes generosity as God's gift to us in the form of eternal life and counsels us to be generous with others. It is through our generosity to others that we are blessed.

- Proverbs 11:24, 25 advises us to be generous and speaks of the rewards of our generosity. *One person gives freely, yet gains even more; another withholds unduly, but comes to poverty. A generous person will prosper; whoever refreshes others will be refreshed.*

- Romans 6:23 describes the free gift of God through Jesus, which is eternal life. *For the wages of sin is death, but the gift of God is eternal life in Christ Jesus our Lord.*

- 1 Timothy 6:18-19 says our generosity and good works are a foundation for a truly satisfying life. *They are to do good, to be rich in good works, to be generous and ready to share, thus storing up treasure for themselves as a good foundation for the future, so that they may take hold of that which is truly life.*

- Matthew 6:33 provides us with the directions to obtain God's generosity. *But seek first the kingdom of God and His righteousness, and all these things will be added to you.*

In the Introduction, I chose "light gap" as the precise metaphor for my mission experience in Southern Sudan. A light gap occurs in a rainforest when a large canopy tree dies and falls, and in the tree's absence, shafts of light penetrate deep into the interior of the forest floor where limited light has been. The light gap facilitates a hothouse of new life, as plants compete for the nutrients provided by the fallen canopy tree and take advantage of the many possibilities for growth the light offers. Like the canopy tree dying, things within me had to die, such as many of my preconceived notions of missionary life and some long-held judgments. The people I met and the things I learned on the other side of the world served as my "light gap" by providing opportunities for discovery and understanding about myself, others and God.

When a friend read the manuscript for *Lessons from Afar*, she told me she had another idea about how the term light gap was a metaphor for the mission experience. "You and Jim were a light gap for the students at Hope and Resurrection Secondary, Mary. I think a light gap can also stand for the caring and compassion that we give others."

In considering the idea of a light gap as it applies to caring for people and ministries, I turned to Matthew 5:14-16: *"You are the light of the world. A city set on a hill cannot be hidden; nor does anyone light a lamp and put it under a basket, but on the lampstand, and it gives light to all who are in the house. "Let your light shine before men in such a way that they may see your good works, and glorify your Father who is in heaven."*

Now re-visit my friend's observation that the metaphor of the light gap in a rainforest represents the caring and compassion we give others. Ask yourself, "What does it mean to my life, if it is true that I am a light gap in the world, and it is the light of Jesus Christ that is shining through me?"

Relating the chapter's theme to your life: Think of the people in your life that live in ways that they are lights in the world. What are some attributes of someone whose light shines before others?

CHAPTER 7

QUESTIONS AND ACTIVITIES

If you are meeting with a group, take turns relating your personal story to one another that answers the following question. If you are reading on your own, record your story in your notebook.

Relating the chapter's theme to your life: Think of the people in your life that live in ways that they are lights in the world. What are some attributes of someone whose light shines before others?

Chapter 7 explores the idea that each of us can be a part of God's mission in the world no matter what our life circumstances are. When our light shines forth into the world, we glorify God. Living in ways that reflect God's love creates a life filled with caring relationships and meaningful purpose and is characterized by generous doses of gratitude and hopefulness.

Micah 6:8—He has shown you, O mortal, what is good. And what does the LORD *require of you? To act justly and to love mercy and to walk humbly with your God.*

Matthew 19:26

Matthew 5:14-16—*"You are the light of the world. A city set on a hill cannot be hidden; nor does anyone light a lamp and put it under a basket, but on the lampstand, and it gives light to all who are in the house. "Let your light shine before men in such a way that they may see your good works, and glorify your Father who is in heaven.*

Part 1

Record your insights in your notebook:

- Re-read Micah 6:8 and Mathew 5:14-16. What connections do you see between the two passages?
- In what ways do the connections that you make between the two verses influence your life circumstances and choices?

Part 2

The final activity is writing an autobiographical poem using the insights gained from reading the seven chapters of this book. Your poem will be a snapshot of your thoughts and reflections. It is helpful to review the themes of *Lessons from Afar:*

Chapter 1 – Discerning present and future "calls" of service.

Chapter 2 – Recognizing fears and the turning over of those fears to God.

Chapter 3 – Acknowledging the mindful practices that support your ideals and principles and help you connect with God and others.

Chapter 4 – Visualizing your "village" of support and care and the consideration of how you can pray for those in your village.

Chapter 5 - Inviting God to be with you in the challenges of your life so that you can soar on wings like eagles as Isaiah 40:31 tells us.

Chapter 6 – Examining our judgments that are negative and result in an attitude of self-righteousness.

Chapter 7 – Claiming the promise from Matthew 5:14-15 that we are the light of the world and that our light shines before men to glorify God.

Directions: Each line of the poem begins with a prompt that mirrors one of the themes of the chapters in *Lessons from Afar*. Using the beginning words for each line, write a statement that reflects some of the self-knowledge and understanding of God you gained. Add description and details to the lines of your poem. Be playful and go with your first thoughts

Template for "I Am Poem":

I am (your name and to whom are you related—perhaps up to three or so relationships)

I am called (a present or future call of service. It can be specific or general that addresses a call to family, church, career, organization, cause, or ideal)

I am afraid (can be either tangible or an idea or emotion of something you fear)

I am mindful of God when (a situation or place that allows you to be aware of God's presence)

I am appreciative of (some of the people who are part of your care and support)

I am seeking God's guidance (your challenges, concerns, opportunities)

I am choosing to be more patient or accepting about (negative things that take your time and energy)

I am the light of Christ because (some belief or way that God's light shines from you)

The author's example of her "I Am Poem"

I am Mary, daughter of Henry and Phyllis, wife of James, and mother of Matthew and Mark.

I am called to assist my faith communities in practical and prayerful ways.

I am afraid of disappointing others.

I am mindful of God when I am in nature, especially observing the first pale golden light of the day.

I am appreciative of my husband Jim who came with me to the other side of the world.

I am seeking God's guidance in this life's season that makes me an elder and ask for the grace to realize the opportunities that this season offers.

I am choosing to be more patient with people who are not good listeners and those who are chronic complainers.

I am the light of Christ because I believe that with God all things are possible.

Sharing your poem when working on your own: If you are working on your own, choose a friend or family member with whom you can share your poem. If you are working in a group, there are two ways in which your poem can be shared with those in your group.

Sharing the poems in a group: The poems can be shared with the group in two ways. The first way is if the group is small, each person can read aloud their poem with the option of leaving out any lines that feel too personal and that he or she is uncomfortable sharing.

The recommended way to share poems:

1. In a circle, each person reads aloud his or her first line about whom they are related. Going clockwise around the circle keeps a sense of order.

2. When everyone in the circle has read the first line of his or her poem, then the first person who shared reads aloud one of his or her favorite lines. Each, in turn, reads a favorite line moving around the circle. The reading around the circle is done without comment or stopping.

3. Again, coming to the person who first began, he or she reads the last line which begins "I am the light of Christ because…" and each, in turn, reads this line from his or her poem.

4. End with an Amen.

The advantage of sharing the poems this way is that hearing one line at a time from each person facilitates being present in listening and weaves the ideas and images into a tapestry of that represent the whole group.

After reading *Lessons from Afar*, writing your reflections in your journal, and creating the "I Am Poem" how would you answer the following question?

If you are the light of the world, and the light shining through you is the light of Jesus Christ, what does that mean for your life today, tomorrow, next month and ten years from now?

APPENDICES

A BRIEF BACKGROUND
AND TIMELINE

Hope and Resurrection Secondary School in Southern Sudan was founded by Darryl and Jennifer Ernst. Darryl and Jennifer were inspired by the friendships with Lost Boys, refugees from Southern Sudan who settled in the Richmond, Virginia area. Hope for Humanity was established to raise money to build the secondary school and to co-administer and financially support the school's operation. To visit the website of Hope for Humanity go to www.hopeforhumanityinc.org

    The village of Atiaba where Hope and Resurrection Secondary is located in the interior of the country about 30 miles from Rumbek and 234 miles from Juba. The school opened with the first class of freshman in 2008 and each following year added a level until in 2011 all four classes from freshmen to seniors were represented. Hope and Resurrection Secondary is co-educational and serves about 250 students per school year. The school year runs from March through December with a break in

August. When the school was opened, there were no university trained secondary teachers in South Sudan, so the teaching staff was recruited from Uganda except for the headmaster, who is South Sudanese. In 2017, the first South Sudanese university trained teacher joined the staff.

The commitment of the Board of Hope for Humanity is *to develop the future leaders of South Sudan through providing educational opportunities.*

❖ 2004 - A nonprofit organization, Hope for Humanity, is founded by Darryl and Jennifer Ernest of Richmond, Virginia to raise funds to build a secondary school in Southern Sudan.

❖ 2007 - The school is built with two buildings of ten classrooms and latrines.

❖ 2008 - The school opens under the direction of Episcopal volunteer missionaries, Jim and Mary Higbee. The school begins with a full-time staff of four and a freshman class of approximately 60 students. Teachers' quarters are constructed.

❖ 2009 - The school's administrative staff is comprised of a Southern Sudanese headmaster and a Ugandan deputy headmaster. The 2008 freshman class is promoted to sophomores, and a new incoming freshman class begins.

❖ 2010 – The school has three class levels represented from freshman to juniors.

❖ 2011 - The school has a staff of eight teachers and two administrators and all levels of classes from freshman through seniors. The first-class graduates.

❖ 2012 - The school has a staff of nine teachers and two administrators. The second-class graduates.

❖ 2013 – One-third of the student population are girls. A dormitory is built for girls so that they can stay at the school. The third-class graduates.

❖ 2014 - The military coup in December 2013 causes concern that the Hope and Resurrection Secondary School cannot open in the spring of 2014. The Ugandan teaching staff agrees to return, and the school re-opens and students have a successful year. Forty percent of the student population is girls. The fourth-class graduates.

❖ 2015 – The concern over the unresolved fighting between military factions continues, but despite unrest and episodes of violence, the school year proceeds as usual with a record number of students registered. The fifth class of students graduates.

❖ 2016 – The school opens with 261 students. Forty percent of the student population is girls. A partnership begins with the Catholic Diocese of Rumbek which provides on-the-ground assistance in obtaining supplies. A Peace Conference is hosted at Hope and Resurrection with secondary students from area schools in attendance. The sixth-class graduates.

❖ 2017 – This year marks the tenth school year of Hope and Resurrection and the seventh-class to graduate. A South Sudanese trained teacher joins the staff.

❖ 2018 – The eleventh school year begins in March. One of the first female graduates of Hope and Resurrection joins the staff in an administrative role.

FACILITATOR'S GUIDE

In the Introduction to the book, the question is asked: Can the lessons that God and the Dinka people of Southern Sudan taught to me be brought home to the United States and applied here for a life that is more abundant and generous?

Ask the question another way: Are the lessons shared in the book about trust, vulnerability, humility, perseverance, and non-judgment limited to mission experiences on the other side of the world, or are the lessons timely and relevant to us who live in developed countries? Readers are invited to answer that question for themselves through thinking, praying, writing and discussing the Bible verses, questions, and activities based on the themes of the seven chapters.

Suggestions for an individual working on his or her own – The format for small groups can be followed when reading and reflecting independently. Journaling responses to the questions is an excellent way to record thoughts and insights.

Suggestions for small group study: Each member of the study group reads the assigned chapter prior to meeting together, but the questions and activity following the chapter are done in the time provided during the class meeting. By providing time in class for answering the end-of-chapter questions, the participants only need to have read the week's chapter before coming to class. The class time provided to reflect and write responses to the activity and questions is followed by a time of whole group discussion and sharing. The pace of each class is one chapter per meeting. The book offers seven chapters which equals seven sessions. Each class session includes the following:

- Opening prayer.
- The check-in question for the week entitled "Relating the chapter's theme to your life."
- Introductory remarks about the current week's chapter and reading aloud the Bible verses and questions or activity for the chapter.
- Individual quiet time to reflect and journal.
- Group sharing of insights after reflecting on the end-of-chapter questions and activities.
- Closing prayer.

Suggested time management for an hour and a half meeting:

Gathering and opening prayer – 5 minutes

Check-in question – 25 minutes (about one-third of the meeting time)

Reading aloud questions, activity directions, and accompanying text – 10 minutes

Quiet time for reflection and writing in notebook – 20 minutes

Whole group sharing of insights – 20 minutes

Closing prayer – 5 minutes

Suggested time management for an hour meeting:

Gathering and opening prayer – 5 minutes

Check-in question – 15 minutes

Reading aloud questions and activity directions and accompanying text – 10 minutes

Quiet time for reflection and writing in notebook – 10 minutes

Whole group sharing of insights – 10 minutes

Closing prayer – 5 minutes

Materials needed: A copy of *Lessons from Afar* and a dedicated notebook or journal to record reflections and answers.

First meeting: To complete the book and activities and questions in seven weeks, the participants will need to have a copy of the book before the first small group meeting and have the Introduction and Chapter 1 read when they come to the first meeting. If it is not possible for participants to have the book before to the first meeting, the Introduction and Chapter 1 can be read out loud at the first meeting and the time for the activity shortened.

Group Norms: At the first meeting, discuss and agree on group norms. Some things the group might consider are being on time to class meetings, coming prepared, and most important, honoring the confidential nature of others' sharing of personal information.

Check-in questions: The check-in question which will begin the weekly study is entitled "Relating the chapter's theme to your life." We do not always have the place and audience to share our personal stories of transformation and faith. The value in sharing our stories and hearing the stories of others is affirmation for the events that comprise our life journey and an increased compassionate understanding of others. Therefore, the check-in question is about the telling of personal experiences regarding the chapter's theme. Because these questions are more thought-provoking than most check-in questions and are an integral part of the reflections and sharing, the question is provided at the end of the chapter, so participants have some time to think about it before coming to class. About one-third of the meeting time is used for the check-in question because of the connections that are made to the theme of the chapter.

Beginning each meeting with personal stories that relate to the theme serves as a bridge from past experiences to being able to think deeply about the questions and activities that relate to the present circumstances of the class members' lives. As the facilitator, you will want to monitor the time so that everyone can share. It is helpful, especially if your group is large, to mentally calculate about how much time each person is allotted for sharing his or her story, and before the sharing begins, letting the participants know the approximate time they each have to answer the check-in question. In groups larger than ten, you may want to divide people into smaller groups of three or four for sharing, so that everyone gets to tell his or his story.

Suggestions for guiding members of the group in how to use the quiet, reflective time: This study provides a quiet, reflective time within the meeting time. The study is designed this way to accommodate the busy lives that most of us lead which often don't provide very much time for being reflective about spiritual matters. Preparation for each week's class is reading the chapter and thinking about the check-in question. Depending on the activity or questions for a chapter, participants may not finish the entire activity or have time to journal on every question. Assure members that it is okay if they do not finish entirely. Suggest that the members of your group start with the question that seems to be the most challenging because insights can be gained by tackling a question that requires deep searching. Encourage members of the group to finish the questions not completed in class during the coming week.

Suggestions for group sharing following the quiet, reflective time: The richness of a small group is the fellowship of others who are also seeking a closer relationship with God. Depending if the class is an hour or an hour and a half, spend time near the end of the meeting for the members of the group to share their insights.

Opening and closing prayer: Prayers from various sources can be used to open and close the meeting. As the group is comfortable with one another, an extemporaneous prayer that addresses the needs of the members is meaningful. You may want to ask different people to lead opening and closing prayer by asking them the week ahead so that they can prepare.

ACKNOWLEDGEMENTS

In writing *Lessons from Afar*, I experienced the words in Hebrews 10: 24-25 in tangible ways through the encouragement of many. *And let us consider how we may spur one another on toward love and good deeds, not giving up meeting together, as some are in the habit of doing, but encouraging one another...*

My first readers were Linda Johnson, Lisa Sargent, and Sally Wayland, and they affirmed that I had a story to tell and that the story had a purpose beyond myself. Reverend Elizabeth Armstrong gave me good advice on the structure of the book. My rector, Reverend Sean Cox, read an early draft and discussed with me the theological ideas that I share in *Lessons from Afar.* Jennifer Ernst never doubted for a minute that I could write this book, and her confidence in me supported my dream of bringing *Lessons from Afar* to completion.

The Wednesday morning Memoir Writing Group in Folsom, California provided a weekly audience to critique excerpts from the book. Their questions revealed where more explicit explanations and information were needed. The facilitator of the writing group, Linda Holderness, gave me professional feedback based on her experience as a journalist and ideas for a book cover.

Life coach, Marie Highby, asked me questions about audience and purpose that brought a new focus to my writing. The Executive Director

Acknowledgements

of Hope for Humanity, Suzanne Hicks, suggested additional ways that the book could be used for Christian formation study groups. Craig Johnson's generous sharing of his expertise in publishing books was invaluable, and his gift of a design for a book cover provided a visual image to represent my hopes of publishing *Lessons from Afar*. Thank you, Craig.

Two study groups at Faith Episcopal Church in Cameron Park, California piloted the study materials found in *Lessons from Afar*. Their perceptive comments and wholehearted participation let me test drive, so to speak, the activities and questions for each chapter. Thank you to all who participated in the study groups for helping me refine my material.

I am grateful for my husband and missionary partner, Jim Higbee, for his wisdom and generosity. Jim's belief that I needed to tell the story of Hope and Resurrection Secondary, and the addition of his memories and ideas made the writing of this book collaborative and satisfying.

Thank you to everyone who asked me how the book was progressing because you kept me motivated and accountable. Jim and I appreciate the continued prayer and financial support of friends and family for Hope and Resurrection Secondary in Atiaba, South Sudan.

Hope and Resurrection Secondary

Atiaba, South Sudan

Matthew 19:26

Made in the USA
San Bernardino, CA
17 April 2018